Small Towns and Regional Development

Dedication

This book is dedicated to
My revered Father

Late Professor Mahinath Jha

Ex HOD PG Department of Maithili
Ram Krishna College, Madhubani (Bihar)

Small Towns and Regional Development

Dr. Vinay Nath Jha

RAJESH PUBLICATIONS
NEW DELHI-110 002

Small Towns and Regional Development

ISBN : 81-85891-64-8

Published by :
M.L. Gupta
Rajesh Publications
1, Ansari Road, Darya Ganj,
New Delhi - 110002

Typesetting by :
Sanjay Gupta
Sanjay Enterprises
New Delhi- 110 002

Printed in India at :
Rajdhani Printers, Delhi -6

Ist Published in India : 2006

RAJESH PUBLICATIONS
Rs. 500.00

Contents

Foreword

The process of urbanization is now more rapid and massive and effects a greater part of the world than ever before, mainly because it is now rampart in the less developed countries which still board three fourths of world's people. The same is true for India, where registrar general is recently released report for the year 2005 highlighted that overall 30% of the population migrated in 2004-05 and the trend is on the rise. The unprecedented rates of overall population growth are helping along with rural-urban migration to swell the population of individual cities more rapidly than ever before. Necessarily, Social, economic and political problems of major significance are being created by huge rural-urban migration and the rapid rise of megapolis, whose main orientation has until recently been agriculture.

'Decentralised Urbanization' and balanced urban growth have often been advocated by developmental planners, who lay emphasis as resticting the growth of metropolitan centres and developing small towns. Recently the government of India has also shown greater interest in promoting growth of small towns to redistribute urban population and reduce polarisation in the settlement pattern of India with its primate city spatial system.

The importance of small town is highlighted by the very fact of congenial setup for a synthesis between the rural-urban strands of contemporary Indian settlement structure. Given the diversities of India and great differences in regional development and regional disparities, the small towns restrain migration streams to large urban centres and act as growth and service centres for the rural hinterland. So the programs to stimulate the development of small towns have been proposed to enable them to perform the role of market centres for rural hinterland in the context of balanced development for the whole district and region.

Small towns accentuate commercial agriculture, create off-farm employment opportunities, diversity rural economies and increase the access of rural people to town based services and facilities. They spread the benefits of urbanization and help in distributing industries throughout the country. Many scholars spine that government must emphasize the substantial resources of to strengthen small towns. It is contended that national government must commit their substantial resources to strengthing small town through top-down planning as well as by mobilizing investment in social and physical infrastructure in rural market centres to facilitate 'bottom up' development. Recent figures of migration as released by Registrar General of India that majority (53%) population migrated from rural to rural areas in the annual year 2004-05 is a start in this direction.

The present book on small towns and regional development is a sincere attempt in this direction to analyse the role of small towns in regional development planning of North Bihar Plain. The region is largely agricultural which is subsistence in nature. It is characterised by poor agricultural base which produce neither enough food for its rapidly growing population nor raw materials for its industry. The region is industrially backward, agriculturally undeveloped with lopsided economy. Riverine ecology and low lying warshy lands dominate the physical landscape. There is complete absence of mineral resources with inadequate transport development. The region is one of the most densely populated parts of India which warrants our attention with respect to the provision of services and commodities. Twenty seven small towns present a shabby look of unplanned growth and also lack employment opportunities and infrastructure incentives. The author is of the view that lack of infrastructure and non-active participation of the people in the economic growth together with apathy of the state govt. are the basic constraints of economic development in the region. The last chapter discusses town own-oriented resource based regional planning, emerging pattern of small towns, examines the strategies for planning and indicates the direction in which small towns may be developed as centres of viable units of growth. These towns have great economic opportunities which will absorb migrants from rural areas and check the drain of migrants destined to bigger cities. The role of small towns in the overall economic structure is low and it is hoped that they have increased role to play in the development like agriculture, agro-based industries and building up of infrastructures, Similarly, there is ample scope for development of industries, food products, fruits and cash crops, in addition to renovation of the sick mills. Thus, development of small towns may promote economic growth with social equity in rural areas.

This book is illustrated with 24 neatly drawn maps and 42 tables. The original material has been rearranged, condensed and thoroughly modified in the light of 2001 census data. Thus, this book takes stock of what we know about pending crises and what the prognosis is for the future. Overall, this is a provocative and important reference book for the researchers, planners and administrators.

B. Thakur
Professor of Geography
Delhi School of Economics
University of Delhi
Delhi - 110 007

Preface

In the age of globalisation the relationship of the town to the countryside is a very important feature in equation of the dynamics of regional development. It was with this point in view that the author has conducted the research project on the role of small towns in development planning of a backward and problem-ridden agricultural region.

This book has its origin from approved Ph.D. dissertation entitled "Population Characteristics and the Role of Small Towns in the Development Planning of the North Bihar Plain" submitted by the author to L. N. Mithila University, Darbhanga in 1997. The original material has been rearranged, condensed and thoroughly modified in the light of 2001 census data.

Over 90 percent population of North Bihar Plain is dependent upon agriculture and high proportion of 79 percent of the total land is cultivated. Large proportion of cultivated land in the region is potentially very productive. However, the abject poverty of this region is itself quite distressing and mind bogging. Despite being predominantly agricultural in character, agriculture at present is incapable to sustain its teeming millions. Qualitative aspects of population viz, literacy, age and sex composition, work force structure, population movement, etc. in the region are symptomatic of grave extent socio-economic malaise which constitute both as a cause and effect of rural backwardness.

Overcrowding and relative economic distress in the region have, therefore, created conditions for considerable male excessive labour migration from the region. With such an immense rural manpower the region provides best opportunities for small towns to grow. The small towns have therefore to prepare themselves to seek the streams of people from rural to urban areas and make appropriate atmosphere for balanced development of the region.

Growth centres and small towns continue to be treated in

isolation from the surrounding hinterland, which depends on services provided by the small towns and which, in turn, is a part and parcel of the local regional economy.

This book is illustrated with 26 neatly drawn maps 7 models, 42 tables, etc. and further gives the summary result of different aspects of development. Notwithstanding, considered opinion and constructive suggestions received from the readers will be of immense volume and the author will be too glad to acknowledge the same.

This work has been completed under the sweet guidance and supervision of Professor K. K. L. Das, Head of the University Department of Geography, L. N. Mithila University, Darbhanga and my teacher Professor N. Sharma, former H.O.D Geography, L. N. Mithila University, Darbhanga whom author is highly indebted. A wide-ranging discussions with them had a profound influence on the final preparation of the book. I am grateful to Professor Baleshwar Thakur, former Vice-Chancellor, L. N. Mithila University, Darbhanga for kindly writing a Foreword to this book. It was a pleasure to have often discussed with him the basic themes outlined in the book, which he very generously offered. I also remember with gratitude all the encouragement and help given by my teachers, friends, fellow students, colleagues of Geography Department, MLSM, College, Darbhanga. I feel pleasure to acknowledge my class friend Sri Dilip Kumar Jha (Bihar Police Service) and Sri Pankaj Kumar Mishra M.A. (Sulabh International Service) while residing at Patna during the collection of data for manuscript.

I shall fail in my duty if I do not express my gratitude to all officials, villagers, small towns notified area authorities, directorate, census operation, Bihar who have extended their co-operation at some stage or other. It is impossible to mention them individually.

I am deeply indebted to my revered father (Late) Professor Mahinath Jha who left us this year. But for his opportune rebukes and the valuable assistance whenever I faltered, the work could not have been expedited. I express my sincere gratitude to my mother Smt. Mahipriya Devi and Grand Mother Smt. Uma Devi, who inspired me always during the completion of work. I also reserve the right to thank my brothers Sri K. N. Jha (A.B.M. Central Bank of India) and Sri. L. N. Jha, lecturer of Chemistry and families whose anxiety and eagerness to see this work completed reflects their love and affection for me. No word of thanks or gratitude can be enough to reciprocate these feelings.

I woe sincere thanks to my beloved wife Smt. Bubu Kumari Jha who kept me aloof from the drudgery and agony of domestic responsibilities and also extend thanks to my loving son Mr. Nitish Kashyap and daughter Ms. Shalini Bharti for keeping peaceful atmosphere during the completion of this project.

I am also thankful to Sri Mohan Lal Gupta, M/s. Rajesh Publications, New Delhi, for undertaking the work of publication, of this book and displaying keen interest in bringing it out within stipulated time limit.

Place : Darbhanga **Dr. Vinay Nath Jha**
Date : 1st January, 2006

List of Maps and Diagrams

List of Tables

List of Abbreviation

Abbreviation	Full Form
T.S.A.	Total Sown Area
F.O.	Frequency of Occurence
L. Q.	Location Quotient
P.I.R.I.	Population Integration Rating Index
S.I.	Size Index
S.C.	Serviceability Score
C.C.	Centrality Score
U.P.R.	Urban Population of Region
U.S.I.	Urban Size Index
G.I.	Growth Indices
S.R.	Sex Ratio
S.C.	Scheduled Caste
I.D.	Index for Differential
U.M.L.R.	Urban Male Literacy Rate
U.F.L.R.	Urban Female Literacy Rate
T.C.P.O.	Town & Country Planning Organisation
N.G.J.I.	National Geographical Journal of India
A.P.G.I.	Association of Population Geographers of India
V	Variables
P.I.N.	Proportionate Index Number
N.I.C.U.	National Information Centre Unit
N.A.G.I.	National Association of Geographers of India
J.R.S.	Journal for Regional Studies
I.R.D.P.	Integrated Rural Development Programme.
P.M.R.Y.	Prime Minister Rojgar Yojna
N.A.B.A.R.D.	Nationalised Bank for agriculture and Rural Development.
A.A.A.G.	Annals of Americal Association of Geographers
GIS	Geographic Information System.

Glossary of Local terms

Aghani	Paddy, Kharif Crops
Rabi	Dalhan Wheat Crop
Bhadai	Monsooni Crop
Garma	Kinds of Paddy
Diara	Area near Big river
Litchi Shahi	A type of Litchi
Makhana	Waterburry
Chaur	Lower Field
Khadi-Handloom	Traditional Handmade Cloth
Mandi	Big Agricultural Produce Market
Haat	Open, Weekly or Biweekly Market in Rural Areas

Chapter-I
Introduction

Conceptual Framework and Rationals of Study:

'**Rural**' and '**Urban**' are two forms of settlement. The dominant functional traits cause settlement to be identified as '**rural and urban categories**'.[1] The swelling proportion of urban dwellers witnessed the first stage with the association of 'Agricultural Revolution' and the proportion reached the new and vigorous dimension as associated with "**Industrial Revolution**".

After Independence, Urban development in India has been accepted as a trend of socio-economic development at large. The rationale of this trend has been taken as tools to examine through demographic characteristics and the role of small urban centres in rural transformation of less developed regions and backward areas.[2]

In consequence, process and pattern of urbanisation, the rapid growth of large urban centres and stagnation or even declining tendency of small towns have been observed as the most obvious trend. Recent trend of the process of excessive metropolitanisation through the growth of huge urban agglomeration and the reverse trend of small towns have brought a hierarchical imbalance in the size distribution of urban centres. The stagnation of small towns in growth perspective has tendend to restrict the diversification of development processes. Urban policy therefore must be oriented to creating networks and nodes which will transform our traditional agriculture into a modern commercial farming and which will create conditions for the development of medium and small scale industries in smaller urban centres.

In the present study, towns having less than 20,000 inhabitants, are recognised as small towns and thus include in them class IV, Class V and Class VI categories of towns of the Indian census, The importance and need of the study lie in imparting integrated development of the economy of the least developed region of North Bihar plain. The small towns are most intimately integrated with the rural areas, providing them with most of the services and commodities, thus functioning as the lowest level of urban service centres. Equally significant is the role of small towns in providing stepped linkages in the chain of interactions between the rural areas and the higher order of urban centres.

Keeping in view the above concerns the key questions which are to be examined include, the specific traits of spatio-temproal behaviour of urbanisation, correlation between urbanisation, economic development and demographic characteristics, existing and estimated potentiality of resource of small urban centres and their re-evaluation including resource mobilisation at different regional scales and the role of small towns and urban centres in wiping out regional imbalances on the basis of town oriented resources by urban-regional planning.

Small towns, larger in number (27) and widely distributed in the study-area, have been accepted as the centres of development. Their development, in general will result in developmental activities closer to rural areas. The relevance of the present study pertains largely to the government policy (plan period 1978-83) to accelerate rural development and simultaneous development of small and medium size towns. It also follows the guideline of ministry of works and Housing (Govt. of India)[3] in which suggestions have been made to plan the towns on the basis of : (i) the natural endowment, (ii) the historical heritage and (iii) the improvement of overall environment of this town. Recent urban planning policy[4] also aims at reversing the growth pattern of urban centres so that the small towns grow rapidly and the large ones either grow slowly or preferably stop growing.

Thus, the locational and the distributional qualities of urban centres in terms of their number, size and centrality have been considered to bear the consequence of regional implications. In view of the tendency of imbalanced urban growth, the need of a proper direction of urban centres at different hierarchies has been felt. Small towns have accordingly been considered to play a vital role in effectuating the condition of urban regional continuum. The development of such centres will certainly bridge the gap between large urban centres and rural areas. The widespread locations of small towns and their possible propensity to grow are supposed to provide the centres a base to become the viable units of growth foci to effectuate the most needed balanced urban-regional growth. In the context of Indian conditions, a five-tier hierarchy of growth foci is observed: (i) Growth Poles, (ii) Growth Centres, (iii) Growth Points, (iv) Service Centres and (v) Central village.[5]

These elements of urban regional development have been examined in depth through various angles in the context of North Bihar Plain and the task for the purpose has been oriented as the integrated development of small towns of the region under study.

Scope of Study:- North Bihar Plain has been taken to form the universe of the study for the present purpose which is a macro regional unit of the state region of Bihar lying wholly to the north of the river Ganga. It is to be emphasized that the modern geography seeks to analyse and interpret an intricate relationship between man and land both in space and time. As any such analysis in abstract terms for the earth as a whole is neither feasible nor desirable, it is necessary to present a systematic interpretation of small areal units. As Hartshorne puts,".. the face of the earth may be thought as made up of a mosaic of individual landscape or regions."[6] Geographers have, of late, arrived at the conclusion that the regional approach to present day analytical geography is not only practicable but also desirable and indispensable. Dickinson,[7] Woolridge & East[8], Davis [9] Stamp [10], Hartshorne [11] and many others have emphatically put forward the case for a regional study. Spate etal have argued that " Regions do exist and even they did not, they would have to be invented to obtain manageable units of study.[12] This is equally pertinent in the case of the study of an area such as the North Bihar Plain where population-land characteristics cannot be fully appreciated unless regional differentiation is made in the right earnest.

An almost rectangular region of North Bihar Plain falls within the geographical extent from 25^{0} 15' to 27^{0} 31' North latitude and 83^{0} 45' to 87^{0} 27' East longitude over the state region of Bihar. The region is bound by international boundary of Nepal in the North, State boundaries of Uttar Pradesh in the West and West Bengal in the east and the holy river Ganga in the South: It comprises whole of the newly re-organised districts of Paschimi Champaran, Purbi Champaran, Gopalganj, Siwan, Saran, Sitamarhi, Muzaffarpur, Vaishali, Madhubani, Darbhanga, Samastipur, Begusarai, Saharsa, Madhepura, Purnea, Araria, Kishanaganj, Katihar, and Naugachia Sub-division of Bhagalpur district. The region thus covers an area of about 53798 sq. Km. and has a population of over 40 million with a density of about 760 persons per km^2 according to 1991 census. The area under study is a least developed macro region of Bihar which itself has since long earned the dubious connotations of being one of the 'least urbanised', least industrialised,' and least developed among the states of the union of India. It is a backward and problem-ridden agricultural region in a less developed state of Bihar.

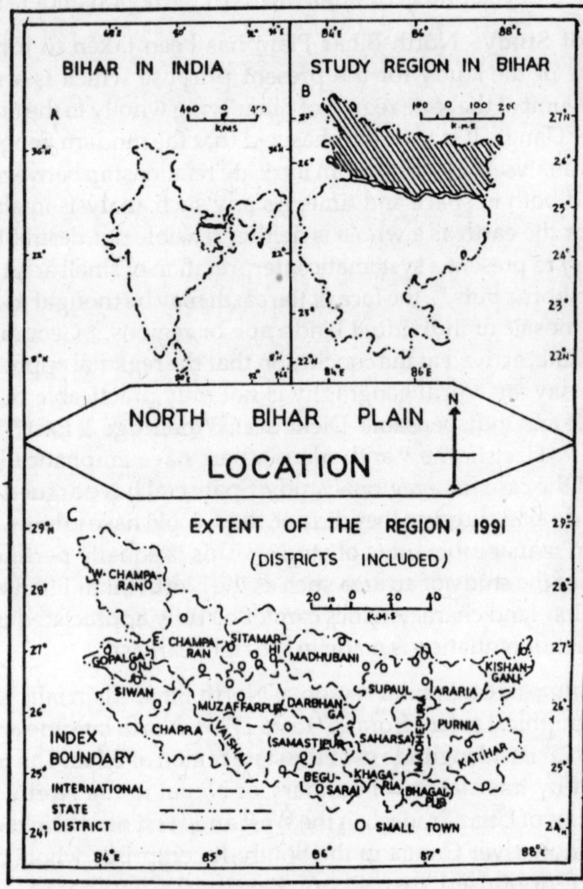

Fig. No. 1 : North Bihar Plain: Location

1A : Bihar in India

1B : North Bihar Plain in Bihar

1C : Extent of the Study Region

Of its population of over 40 millions 29,910,909 persons or about 7.22 per cent live in urban areas. Though the study region has a massive population base and an extremely high man-land ratio, it stands at a fairly low position in the degree of urbanisation. This low degree of urbanisation needs attention in the sense that it has lower level of urbanisation than the state's average of 13.14 percent of urban population and 15.72 and 21.35 per cent for the other macro regions of state i.e. South Bihar plain and High land Bihar respectively.

The morphological characteristics of the study region are exhibited in its alluvial landscape. It, on the whole is flat, monotonous and remarkably featureless composed of river alluvia. Alluvial morphology of the plain has four fold relations viz. facilitative, permissive, restrictive and prohibitive to various resources as the sequel will show. Agriculture, the sole support of over 90 per cent of the population in the region is further, symptomatic of stagnant economy. The regional economy is lopsided, inflexible and sluggish. It is representative of one of the early settled portions of the Middle Ganga Plain in which pressure of population on land resources is intense[13]. Resources of agriculture and physical conditions of farming are largely conducive for prosperous economy. However, despite being predominantly agricultural in character, there is chronic and acute shortages of food availability in the area.[14] It is, therefore, a major stumbling block to development and its inadequacy poses a constant threat to its economic and social stability.

The study, therefore, addresses itself to put new facts and figures designed at solving problems of the backward people in a backward economy. Various stage have been taken viz. :

(i). To make an objective assessment of the physiographic personality of the region together with its restrictive, permissive relationship to agriculture irrigation, transport and communication, human activities.

(ii). To make an inventory of its resources and there by establishing the regional identity.

(iii). To highlight some of the important geo-economic constraints of development, and finally,

(iv) To make recommendations for a rational and pragmatic

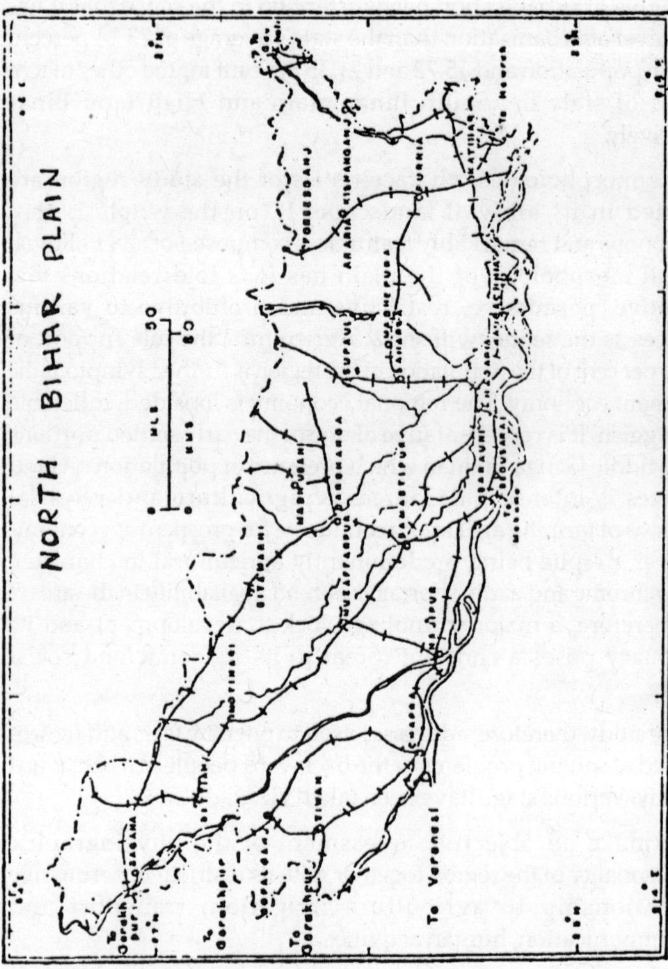

Fig. 1.2 Base Map

development strategy for the economic face-lift of the region

Statement of the problem:

The problem as stated, finds its full reflection in the relevant concept of resource-based urban-regional planning of the North Bihar Plain. It envisages a full understanding of elemental emits of urban centres, their hierarchical planning on the basis of examination of some previous concepts e. g. Christaller, Losch, Thunen etc. their spatial organisation and above all, the concept of integrated development of small towns. Such an orientation will make it possible to fit the findings into State and National conceptual frame work and to make it relevant for practice.

The conceptual framework fits into the approach to justify the contribution of small towns to effect urban-regional planning and their role in the context of rural transformation strategy in a least developed agricultural region through town-oriented resource based technique. This approach has been tried to be reflected through a conceptual model (Fig- 2)

Given the conceptual frame work, the operational issues of the present research project necessitate the inquiries into relevant questions and the formulation of workable hypothesis. Some of the notable questions underlying the proposal include:

(i) What are the existing state of affairs of small towns e.g. social, economic, cultural and demographic characteristics in the area under study ?

(ii) Are there some specific traits of spatio-temporal behaviour of small towns which differentiate them from those elsewhere both at regional and national levels ?

(iii) What are the existing impact of small towns on the economy of the region ?

(iv) Are small towns of the region resource oriented and does their potentiality need to be re-evaluated ?

(v) What areal variations in the role of small towns on over all economic characteristics are significant ?

(vi) Are small towns of the region resource oriented and does their potentiality need to be re-evaluated ?

(vii) To what extent are the functional and other characteristics of existing small towns related to their growth and spatial distribution ?

(viii) Can effective resource mobilization at local level bring development of small towns and check the disproportionate growth of large cities?

(ix) What strategies and proposals for development of these small towns may be suggested to bring desired level of urbanisation and economic development in the region?

(x) Do urban centres of the varying magnitude have hand in bringing overall inequities at different regional seales ?

Given the legacy of all round underdevelopment and examination of the enequities the basic hypothesis of development for the region that seek plausibility may include :

(i) Development strategies for small towns have the possibility to accelerate the pace of town-oriented resource based urban regional planning.

(ii) In a desired urban hierarchy and proportionate growth of varying magnitude of urban centres, planning for the integrated development of small towns which include physical, demographic and socio-economic aspect of regional and sub-regional level has to be weighed.

(iii) Small towns act as filter niche between the large urban centres and rural areas to facilitate the over all regional development, through urban-rural-nexus.

(iv) Existing resource analysis of these urban centres, determines the effective resource mobilisation at regional, sub-regional and local levels.

(v) Small towns can play some effective role in wiping out the regional inequities and rural transformation strategy in a least developed agricultural region of the North Bihar Plain.

It has been sought to achieve these hypothesis through observation, analysis and deliberations on the existing trend and the shape of things to come.

Data Base, Maps and Methodology

Data & Maps :-Types of data collected for this purpose have a wide range from bio-physical to socio-economic. The vastness of the field operation, limited number of hands and the very nature of this research work direct the researcher for secondary sources. Data for the purpose of spatio-temporal behaviour of urbanisation, growth trend of individual urban centres and their resource potentiality have been collected mainly through census publications, i.e. Town Directory, General population Tables, District census Handbooks, Bihar Statistical Handbook, Block Agricultural Statistics Directory. Several statistical publications of the government, including State Planning Board, Report of Directorate of Statistics and Evaluation, Barsik Prativedan published by Govt. of Bihar and published articles and journals from government and other organisations have also been taken into view.

The following categories of maps were made available and have been incorporated in this study:

(i) 1 inch to 16 miles (1:1,000,000), 1 inch to 10 miles (1:633600) and 1 inch to 20 miles (1:1267200) anchal maps of Bihar published by the State Survey Office, Gulzarbagh, Patna.

(ii) 1 inch to 4 miles (1:23440) District maps of the parent districts of Champaran, Saran, Muzaffarpur, Darbhanga, Monghyr and Bhagalpur.

(iii) Various other maps contained in the census Atlas of Bihar, Census Centenary Atlas (1973), General report of the census (1981), Lear month and Bhatta's : An Atlas of Resources (Mysore State), Municipal Office and Notified Area Committee Office, etc. were also consulted and their tracing were made for use in this work.

To Provide a more rational and especially for the preparation of salient land use pattern of small towns of the study area some representative towns have been chosen for detailed study. The information has been collected personally by the author from all the sampled towns in the region.

Cartographic Techniques and Mapping :- The task of data processing and data analysing have formed the final stage of diagnostic research frame. Different techniques of tabulation, calculation, correlation, cartographic representation and map preparation have constituted the essential parts of analysis. The degree and nature of imbalances and their relationship at different levels and the identification of facts have been achieved through analysis of 'Rank', 'Ratios', 'Index of concentration', 'Size Index', 'Spearmans correlation coefficient' and 'Intensities' calculation etc. On the statistical and quantitative methods the application of cartographic techniques such as proportionate circles, bar and line graphs, curves, maps and models have proved helpful in giving the geographic treatment of the study on a sound base.

A map summarises the main points of any description and saves labour and time even in theoretical elaboration. Hartshorne emphatically points out "maps constitute a ready rule of thumb to test the geographic quality of any study which a geographer makes and if the problem can not be studied fundamentally by maps, usually by a comparison of several maps, then it is questionable whether or not it is within the field of geography.[15] maps are the one indispensable tool in geography not only for numbers, but also for other demographic phenomena have been asserted by zelsinky,[16] Stamp[17], Mackenjee and many others.

One of the main problems involved in the planning of maps was the selection of interval between different categories. Still another problem was to select the propen black and white shades in order to represent various categories with distinctive class intervals. For the first purpose, each of them was provided with five to seven categories as "the human eyes can conveniently differentiate this number of steps from black to white [18]. For the second purpose, shades were chosen keeping inview : (1) The absolute values which these shades were to represent and (ii) The range of class intervals. Subjectivity in the preparation of maps, selection of method, class interval and the value size together with location of dots and symbols, etc. has been avoided as far as practicable.

In the method of analysis, therefore, chief elements in the mainstream of this study may be categorised into:

(a) Systematic analysis of maps and representation of statistics by suitable cartographic methods, and

(b) Analysis of data and their correlation and geographic interpretation.

Review of Previous Work Done :- The present research work in corporates all the main components involved in the population characteristics at one hand and the elements of small towns and their related aspects of urbanisation at the other. Naturally, therefore, the themes and area coverage of the undertaken project include the contents of population geography and urban regional planning at one stake. In the continuous changing and improving trend of geographic study and research, the said branches of the mother-discipline of geography have emerged recently as significant sprouts. The largest number of doctorates in geography in India have been in urban geography and population geography.

It is true that the themes and area coverage of present research work are not entirely new. Many researchers have done works which have the objectives partially similar to those of the project, but the study approach to the problems of smalltowns as the centres of development and their role in the rural transformation strategy in the least developed region like the North Bihar Plain is yet to be envisaged. They need be studied particularly from the view point of population and urban geography. The important works are being highlighted in following paragraphs.

In the works Mrs. M. Mukherjee (1976)[19] and S.M. Karimi (1967)[20], the authors have examined, on the basis of some set variables of basic and non basic functions, the functional character of towns and the spatio-temporal behaviour of urban settlement respectively. The Population charectristics and measurement of population pressure in relation to available resources of the North Bihar Plain have extensively been studied in the work of K.N. Das (1969)[21] and K.K.L. Das (1990)[22]. These two works may be regarded as notable efforts towards the applied study approach in population geography.

Similar to the aim of present research, the works of N.. Sharma (1989)[23] and S. N. Jha (1989)[24] may be considered as plansible starts in the right direction. The case and role of medium size towns and small size towns of Bihar have respectively been established in these works for a desired urban-regional planning strategy in the state. The inventory of possibilities and limitations on the basis of multi-variable analysis and their correlation with relevant facets of development in the state have rationally been viewed in both these works.

Saiyad. S. Safi (1983)[25] lays stress on the selection of towns within the ambit of a state wise urban development strategy for project-formulation, and suggests that programme of action to be tailored in accordance with the topography, specific needs and circumstances of the area. C.S. Chandrashekhara (1983)[26] advocates that the town has to be linked to the hinterland as well as to the next order town in hierarchy within the region.

K.N. Singh (1958)[27] has tried to provide a causative analysis of the reciprocal influences between rural markets and urban centres of eastern U.P. The work is based on certain emperical studies. V.N. Singh's (1986)[28] work on growth foci analysis of North Bihar Plain may also be treated as a good volume containing some precise techniques of regional analysis. The Ph.D. Dissertation of T. Jha (1984)[29] is also a valuable work containing regional information of North Bihar Plain.

K.D. Jha (1993)[30] has studied issues related with urban agglomeration which carry vast implications of development planning both at urban and regional scales in the state of Bihar.

"Place of small towns in India" edited by R.L. Singh and Rana P.B.Singh (1979)[31] contains a number of scholarly papers on small towns by several distinguished authors. They highlight some important findings, viz.:

(i) In relatively backward regions with sporadic development and having contradictory ecological situations, resource localisation is the most responsible factor for the growth, functional structure and location of small towns.

(ii) Topography has negligible role in controlling frequency in the growth of towns.

(iii) Generally small towns on any regional scale, reveal the result of decreasing trend in terms of number population and share in urban population during the past decades.

(iv) In the most cases the spatial distribution of small towns may be treated as 'agropolis' which accelerates energy in transformating rural territory.

Besides these broad research projects, recently a good number of articles have appeared, and they have broad similarities with the aims and objectives of the present research. The list is exhaustive[32] but is very pertinent to be presented in this work can be cf. References cited.

The author had occasions to look into similar works by a band of geographers, economists and others which deal exclusively with population characteristics or analyse regional planning or both. But space does not permit of an elaborate treatment nor review of each work is possible. Besides, in many of the Indian Universities, the Institute of Development Studies and the Centres for Urban and Regional Studies, Mysore, I.C.P.O. New Delhi and Town & Country Planning Organisation, a band of teachers and research scholars are working in the field of urban-regional planning. In Varanasi, Punjab, Patna, Ranchi and many other universities of the country the individual university Department of Geography has done commendable work in this field.

The above review of previous works done reflects the fact that the role of small towns in the rural transformation-strategy of a least developed region like North Bihar Plain is still to be ascertained. Within the densely populated region like North Bihar Plain an examination of the population characteristics with their salient economic facets is needed for any planning strategy. With this perspective, present work attempts to analyse the variable related to salient socio-economic demographic features and role of small towns with the help of their multi-dimensional potentiality for a desired development planning of North Bihar Plain.

Development Ingredients of North Bihar Plain:- According to 1991 census, the North Bihar Plain, having about 17.41 per cent of its work force employed in non-agricultural sector of economy stands as the least industrialised among the three macro regions of Bihar, viz.

1. North Bihar Plain
2. South Bihar Plain and
3. Highland Bihar.

Under the circumstances, any inventory of strategy for development of small towns is to be made only after "cautious search for possibilities and limitations-physical, human, material and developmental climate in general"[33] in the region under study.

Physical Resources :- The morphology of the plain is, to a large extent, dependent on drainage characteristics of a number of Himalayan streams such as the Gandak, Burhi Gandak, Ghaghra, Baghmati and its extension Kareh, Kamla Balan, Bhutahi Balan, Tilyuga, Kosi and the Mahananda. All the streams having north-south or north west-south east trends flow nearly parallel to each other, and on the completion of their journey they empty into the

Ganga in the south. The plain on the whole is monotonous and featureless due to low and imperceptible relief. Topographic features of this vast plain[34] are the paramount importance so far as their application to human settlements and economic activities over the entire plain are concerned. It determines to a large extent, the land use and cropping pattern, transport and communication and influences the very way of life of the people.

The fluvial action of the major streams has shaped the socio-economic fabric of the people in the region. Two facts of paramount importance which have been duly influenced by fluvial morphology of this region and which emerge out in bold relief are: firstly, land resources that are the physical heritage of the past several thousand years; and secondly, the pattern of human settlements that are the direct outcome of the agricultural economic environment. The pristine richness of soil often renewed with fresh river borne silt in course of annual flooding has imparted to the landscape a natural resource- almost unparalleled elsewhere-an asset which has acted as a pull factor for dense human settlements prompting fairly intensive landuse. Physical environment thus as a stimulant for agricultural development is conducive for prosperous farming. The region has a sub-tropical with monsoonal rhythm characterised by a hot dry summer, warm moist rainy season and a cool and dry winter. These climatic conditions have greatly influenced cropping pattern where by four agricultural harvests are obtained annually. The alluvial morphology the plain therefore, needs to be considered as a promising line of approach to regional planning of this backward region.

Human Resources : With 31 Percent of Rural area of the state of Bihar the study region contains over 49 percent of is population in 1991, indicating a high location quotient of 1.61. Its rural population density (716 p/km2) its almost twice the density of Bihar (441) and thrice that of India, which clearly shows the nature and extent of overcrowding in this agricultural belt. This area with very high density of population and immense poverty has been labelled as rural slum[35] and forms that portion of the Middle Ganga Plain where the concentration of population is the greatest.

Further, over a vast population base even a modest percentile increase results in an enormous rise in absolute numbers. Qualitative aspect of population, viz. literacy, age and sex composition, work

Table 1.1

North Bihar Plain

Regional Setting, Area and Population 1991 Figures in bracket represent per cent of total area and population respectively.

Sl. No.	District	Area in Km2			Population in '00				Density/km2	
		Total	Rural	Urban	Total	Rural	Urban	Total	Rural	Urban
1	2	3	4	5	6	7	8	9	10	11
1.	Saran	2461	2577.4	63.6	25730	23386	2344	974	907	3685.8
2	Siwan	2219	2192.98	26.0	21710	20555	1155	978	937	4439.0
3.	Gopalganj	2033	1983.07	49.93	17043	16074	969	838	811	1940.0
4.	Paschim Champaran	5228	5138.43	89.57	23337	20983	2354	446	408	2627.7
5.	Purbi Champaran	3968	3908.60	59.34	30431	28697	1734	767	734	2921.4
6.	Sitamarhi	2643	2596.11	46.89	23915	22580	1335	905	870	2847.2
7.	Muzaffarpur	3172	311.64	55.36	29539	26789	2750	931	860	4966.8
8.	Vaishali	2036	1998.48	37.52	21461	20027	1434	1054	1002	3820.7
9.	Begusarai	1918	1879.88	38.12	18148	16371	1777	946	871	4661.6
10.	Darbhanga	2279	2259.82	19.18	25110	22926	2184	1102	1014	11386.3

11.	Samastipur	2904	2863.48	40.52	27170	25821	1349	936	902	3328.6
12.	Madhubani	3501	3475.76	25.24	28320	27293	1028	809	785	4071.4
13.	Saharsa	4112	4041.98	70.02	24753	23036	1717	602	570	2451.8
14.	Madhepura	1788	1730.64	57.36	11777	11009	768	659	636	133.5
15.	Khagaria	1486	1473.54	12.46	9872	9284	588	664	630	4719.4
16.	Purnia	3229	3148.59	80.41	18789	17207	1581	582	547	1966.6
17.	Araria	2830	2778.93	51.07	16116	15094	14023	569	543	2002.7
18.	Kishanganj	1884	1896.35	47.65	9841	8848	993	522	482	2083.5
19.	Katihar	3057	3021.15	35.85	18254	16538	1716	597	547	4787.1
20.	Naugachia S/D (Bhagalpur Distt.)	238.27	227.03	11.24	1841	1528	312	772.5	673	12780.2
21.	North Bihar Plain	53166	52249	917.35	403154	374045	29109	758	716	3173.1
22.	Bihar	373877	170133.15	3743.85	863745	750215	113530	479	441	3032.4
23.	Regional total as % of State Bihar	3057	30.17	24.5	46.67	49.85	25.64	-	-	-

Source : Compiled from census of India, 1991, Series A-Bihar, Dist. wise Primary census Abstract

force, population movement, etc. in the region is further symptomatic of grave extent socio-economic malaise and stagnant economy and constitute both as a cause and effect of rural backwardness. Overcrowding and relative economic distress in the study area have, therefore, created conditions for considerable male excessive labour migration from the region. With such an inimmense rural manpower, the region provides best opportunities for small towns to grow. The small towns have, therefore, to prepare themselves to soak the streams of people from rural to urban areas.

Material Resources :-The most important material resource of the region is particularly related to land. Being pre-eminently suited to ecological environment duly reinforced by a complete lack of mineral resources this region is par excellence an agricultural tract. Alluvial morphology of the region also influences field pattern, possibilities of irrigation, the size and distribution of holdings, continuity of cultivation and above all, the most important aspect of agriculture, i.e. the crop of their nature, yield and out turn. The plain topography of the region ensures continuity of cultivation assures extensive irrigation facilities because of low gradient and huge surface as well as underground water resources. It further facilitates consolidation of the present small and scattered land holdings as a result of which working on forms becomes easier here than what would obtain in plateau and mountainous relief.

Over 82 per cent of its population is dependent upon agriculture and a high proportion of 79 per cent of the total land is cultivated. Large proportion of cultivated land in the region is highly potentially productive. Many references bear testimony to the fact that agricultural instinct of early settlers of the middle Ganga valley of which the region form a part is thoroughly embodied in the life and culture of the people.[36] However, in the present state of our knowledge the area is poorly served with irrigation facilities (only 21% in NSA) The burden of population on agricultural land is a rule rather than an exception. Agriculture on the whole is primitive, basically subsitance in character whereby cereals predominate (76% of T.S.A.) and cash crops are subsidiary.

Aghani and Rabi harvests are most Important in the region. Their corresponding proportion in T.S.A. are 36 and 33 respectively. They are followed by Bhadai (24%) and Garma (7%) harvests which taken together account for about one third of T.S.A. The influence of alluvial morphology is also clearly discernible in the difference between the cropping pattern of the riverside levee uplands on the one hand and the interfluvial lowlands behind the levees on the other.

Rice, Sugarcane, Maize and Jute are main agricultural products.[37] Sugar is produced mainly in Saran, Siwan, Gopalganj, Purbi Champaran and Paschimi Champaran districts. Rice is grown in almost all districts while maize- in Saran, Siwan, and Gopalganj districts. Jute production is confined mainly in the district of Purnia and Kathihar. In brief, the levees are marked by such crop as maize, sugarcane, bhadai, rice, oilseeds etc. Which prefer well drained conditions. The entire diara tract is pre-eminently suited to growing bumper bhadai and rabi crops with fairly high yields have made the farmers economically more strong than in any other part of the region. One significant point to mention is that bhadai harvest is comparatively less widespread in northern portions as compared to their southern counterparts. Agriculture is intensive as much as the agricultural fields are kept engaged throughout the year so that chance failure of one crop is largely compensated for by another.

Fruits like mango, litchi, banana and potato cultivation need special attention in Tirhut Division. The storage and marketing system may be developed in existing small towns and a few market centres should be developed. There are reasons to believe that future planning can be done scientifically for the benefit of agriculture and the peasantry.

Fisheries and Live Stock Resources:- Pisiculture has been the traditional activity of the region and in primary sector, it may provide additional employment. North Bihar Plain with vast area under water bodies including tanks has enormous potentialities for development of inland fisheries. Thus, it may, in turn, meet the challenge of reducing the number of workers who need be provided with jobs in secondary and tertiary activities.

The concentration of livestock resources is also considerable because the districts of North Bihar Plain are basically agricultural. However, conditions for the production of milk are not of much importance and animal husbandry at the moment, is worst managed. In future, possibility of a few dairy plants may not be ruled out in the region.

A large livestock produce is available in the form of cattle hides, skin and bones in all district of the region. But due to the absence of the related industries, the materials are generally sent to Kolkata and Kanpur for processing and tanning. Due to strategy and planning this field would give a wide scope of development to these industries in this region.

Forest and Minerals Resources-North Bihar Plain is deficient in forest and mineral resources. Potentiality of forest based industries exists in Pachimi Champaran and Purnia districts. In Material resources only sand stones and mud are available. They may help construction activities. However, in Saran, Siwan, Gopalganj district, the availability of nodular limestone and nitrate provide opportunities for developing some industries. Likewise, in the district of Purbi Champaran and Paschimi Champaran, availability of mussel shell will facilitate manufacturing of mother and pearl buttons.

General Developmental Climate:- Among the developmental infrastructures, transport and communication are of much significance as they facilitate the movement of man and materials. In the districts of North Bihar roads and railways are adequately laid to serve the region's development. The lines, however, run parallel to numerous rivers, making the approach between two places tedious and time taking. The influence of topography here is manifest in the peculiarities of operation and structure of short metre gauge railways in the region. Enormous time to cover short distances is another example of adjusting railway engineering to fluvial geomorphology. The geomorphic control on railway is further seen largely as rail lines zone in the hilly area in the extreme north west of the region. Roads are not only inadequate, but are in a large number of cases unmetalled, the eastern section is rather poor in road transportation facilities. The number of metalled roads and their mileage is limited due to high cost of construction. Metalled roads run for short distances, joining the important urban and trade centres of the region. The region only around 12 kms. road for every lakh population as against 60 kms. in other states, and even these roads are in deplorable condition. River navigation may prove a better aid to transport services provided it is utilized effectively. Transport and communication are however not a formidable challenge in the development of the region characterised largely by facilitative geomorphology.[38]

With the expanding network of broad gauge services and construction of National Highway No. 31 which passes through the heart of the region, the area is steadily undergoing socio-economic changes. The construction of "Rajendrapul" over the Ganga river in 1959 has facilitated the extension of broad line in the study region as under.

Sl. No.	BG Conversion From	To	Distance in kms.	Year of Completion
1.	Barauni	Samastipur	51	1962
2.	Samastipur	Muzaffarpur	52	1975
3.	Muzaffarpur	Sonepur	59	1976
4.	Sonepur	Chapra	52	1981
5.	Barauni	Katihar	180	1984
6.	Muzaffarpur	Raxaul	130	1995
7.	Samastipur	Darbhanga	38	1995

This conversion of MG lines to BG lines apart from construction of some other metre gauge lines in the interior parts (Jhanjharpur to Laukaha Bazar) of the region has provided facilities for moving essential traffic to accelerate the developmental activities. However, a great challenge for fulfilling the aspiration of people to provide efficient and sufficient transport facilities needed to cope with the expending activities of agriculture, industries, business, education, tourism, pilgrimage, commuters, factory and office workers, etc. still persists in the region.

It proves an uphill task to tackle them due to lack of adequate funds and resources. Secondly, for a balanced regional development in pursuance of national goal this process has further to gain momentum as there are, aras in the interior which are still vulnerable to menacing floods and remain cut off from their district hadquarters during peack discharge in July and August.

Extremely low per capita temporal consumption of electricity in the region (Table. 1.2) proves as deferrent development constraint and is clearly symptomatic of backward economy. The problem is also of frequent failures and erratic supply of electicity. This is to be looked in to by Bihar State Electricity Board so that industrial development may not be discouraged in the region.

Table 1.2

Temporal Pattern of Region wise per capita Consumption of Electricity in Bihar (in Kwh)

Year	North Bihar	South Bihar	Chotanagpur	Bihar	India
1951	0.42	7.96	71.37	19.80	17.78
1956	1.09	11.12	107.43	29.74	26.40
1960-61	2.53	24.52	141.41	41.09	38.95
1965-66	3.96	30.73	166.76	57.70	61.33
1973-74	11.02	36.94	200.58	71.03	97.48
1975-76	15.07	43.69	237.26	84.11	109.95
1976-77	15.23	44.16	239.82	88.59	119.38
1977-78	15.25	44.23	240.04	87.32	120.73
1978-79	16.60	39.80	284.84	87.46	30.94
1979-80	17.46	43.25	266.64	79.94	130.49
1980-81	14.82	43.40	249.06	74.07	132.34
1981-82	13.43	49.14	240.02	83.21	140.60
1982-83	18.55	62.21	257.37	85.00	146.00
1983-84	18.42	46.26	267.92	84.57	146.00

Source: Bihar State Electricity Board at A Glance, 1983-84, p.15

Creation of enterpreneurship, lacking at present for behind what is desired, is another constraints for industrial development in the region. Observations reveal that enterprinsers hesitate in coming forward due to the lack of proper incentives in the form of financial, banking facilities in particular and lack of tecnhical know-how and law and order problem in general It is, however, encouraging to note that a proper industrial climate is being provided by judicious effort of Directorat of industries, Bihar, Directorate of Technical education, Bihar; different financial agencies and banks by establishing industrial estates, extrending loan facilities an easy terms, providing other infra-structureal assitance like land an opening industrial training centres and a package of incentives. These help to existing industrial unit remove problems of under utilisation and invite new enterprisers to locate new industrial units all over the region in the changed political set up now.

Thus, in the light of development ingredients in view of possibilities and limitation for planning of the North Bihar Plain, It becomes, clear that the region is not fit for the establishment of large and heavy mineral-based industries. The strategies therefore, give emphasis on development of agro resource based and demand-based medium and small scale industries in the region. Both locally, and regionally the study area has high potential for small scale industrialisation of late, it has also earned its fame in the country and abroad for "Mithila Painting" that are lustly enlogised and highly, prized as good specimens of art. Despite all these, the region is industrially more backward than other regions of the state.[39] Due to all these problems the economic situation of the region is gloomy and is further gradually getting involved in a vicious circle as more and more people are added to the already existing large population base marked by stagnant economy. The opt-quoted line '**poverty in the land of plenty" requires a fresh look** at the problem of the area because though endowed with rich resources its people are still depressed.

Format of Chapters:- The present work has been planned to comply with to cover different stages of study in sequential and conclusive frame. The entire study has been covered in altogether eight linked chapters.

Chapter I Introduces the theoretical and emperical framework in which this study is set. It spells out the objectives, problems at hand, approaches, coverage of research, development ingredients of the study area and also reviews the literature in the field.

Chapter-II "Urbanisation: A contemporary Regional Perspective" Incorporates the locational characteristics and patterns of small towns in the region. The geographical and regional location of small towns with reference to their population size and spatial significance in the context of prevailing site and situation has been discussed.

Chapter-III has been planned to assess the growth behaviour of small towns. Observations reveal that these towns fail in acquiring a desired growth. The most obvious trend in growth pattern has been in decline or near stagnation in most cases and whenever there is any symptom of higher population growth rate, it is due to special circumstances like emergence of the centre is recent decade, etc. Small towns present conspicuous decline in the proportion of people living there in to total state's urban population. These aspects have been examined in depth to orient the case of planning strategies for the development of small towns.

Chapter-IV is designed to examine the salient bio-cultural economic characteristics of small towns. An in-depth analysis of age composition, sex-ratio, literacy and their variations among small towns and correlation with other variables of socio economic facets have been made. This is followed by a meaningful discourse on the economic structure and functional behaviour of small towns in the region. The economic character of small towns reveals that they fail in providing a desired functional hierarchy of urban settlement in the region.

Chapter-V forms the most important part of this research work. The multi-variable potentiality and service efficiency of small towns along with the other relevant facts and problems have been studied and analysed. Proposals in the light of broad goal of balanced regional development have been made.

Subsequently, the VI Chapter elaborately discusses emerging pattern of small towns of North Bihar Plain at a future date and also examines the strategies for planning proposals and indicates the direction in which these towns may be developed as centres of viable units of growth foci in the region.

Chapter VII summarises main findings and makes prescriptive recommendations for the development of the region.

At the end, Chapter VIII Regional Population : Contemporary Directions 2001, which enhance the utility and effectiveness of Present Scenario.

References

1. Sharma, N. **1980** Temporal Dimension of Geography Recent Trend and concepts in Geography (ed.) R.B. Mandal and V.N.P. Singh, Concept Publishing Co. New Delhi, p. 13.
2. Mishra, R.B. 1971 Griowth Poles and Growth Centres in Urban and Regional Planning in India, *Development Studies No.*2 Institute of Development Studies, University of Mysore, pp. 10-11.
3. Saiyad, S. Safi 1983 Integrated Development of small and medium towns in Indian Context : Problem and prospect in Integrated Development of small and Medium Towns: Problems and Strategic Policy Issue". (ed.) R.K. Wishwakarma and G. Jha, New Delhi p.81.
4. Planning Commission 1978-83 : " Draft Sixth five year plan, Govt. of India, New Delhi, pp. 222-223.

5. Mishra, R. P. Sundaram, K.V., and Prakash Rao, V.L.S. 1974 : Regional Development Planning in India, A New Strategy, Vikash Publishing House, New Delhi, p.205.

6. Hartshorne, R. 1958 'The Nature of Geography, Lancaster, Pa, p.250.

7. Dickinson, R.E. 1939 "Landscape and Society" *Scott, Geog. Meg.* Vol. 55 Bi, 1, p. 13.

8. Woolridge, S.W. and East, W.W. 1951 The Spirit and Purpose of Geography, London, p. 159.

9. Davis, Kingslay 1951 : The population of India & Pakistan, Princeton, N.J. P. 4.

10. Stamp, L.D. 1960 Our Development World, Faber, London, pp. 14-15.

11. Hartshorne, R. 1958 Op. Cit, p. 293.

12. Spate, O.H.K. and Learmonth, A.T.A. 1967 India and Pakistan, London, p. 140.

13. Das, K.K.L. and Das, K.N. 1992 Agricultural Land use and Pressure of Population" in Spatial Dimension of Agricultue, vol. Five, (ed. Noor Mohammad), Concept Publication Co. New Delhi, pp. 257-63

14. Das, K.K.L. 1998 "Availability of Food grains and Food policy in a Backward Region of North Bihar Plain" in Food System of the World (ed: by M. Shafi and A. Aziz) Rawat Publications, Jaipur, pp. 510-16.

15. Hartshorne, R. 1958 op. cit. p. 249.

16. Zelinsky, W. 1966 "A Prologue to population Geography, Prentice Hall, Englewood Cliff, N.J. p. 6

17. Stamp, L.D. 1960 Applied Geography, Harmourd Worth, p. 192.

18. Robinson, A.H. 1962 Element of Geography, John Wiley & Sons Inc. Newyork, p. 177.

19. Mukherjee, Mos. M. 1966 "Functions and Functional Classification of Towns in Bihar; Ph. D. Thesis, Patna University, Patna.

20. Karimi, S.M. 1967 Urban Settlement in Bihar Plain; Ph. D. Thesis,

Aligarh Muslim University Aligarh.

21. Das, K. N. 1969 Land use Changes in Kosi Region, Bihar; Approved Ph. D. Thesis, Bahagalpur University, Bhagalpur.
22. Das, K.K.L. 1990 Population and land Resources : A Study of North Bihar Plain West of Kosi, Amit Prakashan, Patna.
23. Sharma, N. 1989: Strategies for the development of Medium Size Towns in Bihar : A Study in Developmental Technology, L. N. M. U. Publication, Darbhanga.
24. Jha, S.N. 1989 Small Towns of Bihar : A Study in Urban Regional Planning, Approved PH. D. Thesis, L.N.M.U. Darbhanga.
25. Saiyad, S. Safi, 1983 op. Cit., p. 81.
26. Chandra Shekhar, C.S. 1983 Integrated Development of Small & Medium Towns: Problem & Issues in Perspective," (ed) Vishwa Karma & Jha (Cf. Ref. 3).
27. Singh, K.N. 1958 "Rural Market and Urban Centres in Eastern U.P. : A Geographical Analysis, Ph.D. Thesis, B.H.U. Varanasi.
28. Singh V.N. 1986 Spatial Urban Pattern and Growth of Urbanisation, Inter-India Publications, New Delhi.
29. Jha, T. 1984 North Bihar: A Study in Regional Planning, Approved, Ph. D. Thesis, L.N.M.U. Darbhanga.
30. Jha, K.D. 1993 Urban Agglomeration of Bihar; A Study in Problems of Concentration and Urban Settlement Planning, Approved Ph.D. Thesis, L.N.M.U. Darbhanga.
31. Singh, R.L. & 1979 'Place of Small Towns in India, N.G.J.I. Varanasi.
32. The list of authors with their work:

(i) Hoffer, C.R. 1929 A Study of Town-Country Relationship, East Lansing, Michigan State College, Agricultural Experiment Station, Special Bulletin No. 181.

(ii) Dickinson, R.E. 1932 The Distribution and Functions of Smaller Urban Settlement of East Anglia' *Geography*, Vol. 17, No. 95, Part I, pp. 19-31.

(iii) Hoyt, Homes 1941 Economic Background of cities' Jour. of Land and Public Utility Economics, 17, pp. 188-95

(iv) Brush, J.E. 1953 The Hierarchy of Central Place in South Wisconmm": *Geog. Rev.* Vol. 43.

(v) Clark, P. J. and Evans, F.C. 1954 Distance to Nearest Neighbour as a measure to Spatial Relations", *Ecology*, 35, pp. 445-53

(vi) Berry, B.J.L. and Garrison, W.L. 1958 "The Functional Bases of the Central Place Hierarchy "*Eco. Geog.* Vol. 34, pp. 145-54

(vii) 1958 "Alternative Explanation of Urban Rank-size Relationship", *AAAG* Vol. 48, pp. 83-91

(viii) Webb, J.W. 1959 "Basic Concept in the Analysis of Small Urban Centres in Minnesota", *AAAG*, Vol. 49.

(ix) Berry, B.J.L. and Garrison, W.L. 1961 "City Size Distribution and Economic Development" in Eco. Development and Cultural Change, Vol. 9, pp. 573-88.

(x) Ellefsen, R.A. 1962 City Hinterland Relationship in India" in Roy Turner (ed.) India's Urban Future, California Press, pp. 94-116.

(xi) Breese, G. 1963 "Urban Development Problems in India" AAAG Vol. 53, pp. 253-65.

(xii) Mayfidd, R.C. 1967 "Central Place Hierarchy in Northern India, Punjab", in Garrison, W.L. and Marble, D.F. (eds), Quantitative Geography-I, Economic and Cultural Topics, Evanston North Western University, pp. 120-66.

(xiii) Sinha, K.K. 1968 "The Growth of Towns Along the Ganga in Bihar "*Trans. ICG*, Vol. 5, pp. 149-57.

(xiv) Ahmad, E. 1952 Town Study with Special Reference to India", *Geographer*, Vol. 5, pp. 1-26.

(xv) Ahmed, E. 1956 Origin and Evolution of the Towns of U.P. "*Geog. Outlook*, pp. 38-58.

(xvi) Aziz, A. 1955 "A Study of Indian Towns" *The Geographer*, Vol. 7, pp. 9-18.

(xvii) Dayal, p. 1959 "Population Growth and Rural-Urban Migration in India", *N.G.J.I.* Vol. 5, pp. 179-85.

(xviii) Mukherjee, A.B. 1973 "Small Towns of Uttar Prades" A Explanatory Analysis", *Man Power Journal*, Vol. ix, No. 3, pp. 82-97.

(xix) Jauhari, A.S. 1962 "Growth of Urban Settlements in the Stlej-Yamuna Divide" *NGJI*, Vol. 8 (i), pp. 1-24.

(xx) Singh, R.L. and Singh, K.N. 1963 "Evolution of the Medieval Towns in the Saryupar Plain of the Middle Ganga Valley : A Case Study" *NGJI*, Vol. 9 (i), pp. 1-11

(xxi) Jha, B.N. 1964 "Recent Trend of Urbanisation in Bihar", *Jour. of Ranchi Univ.*, Vol. 2 (4), pp. 35-44.

(xxii) Singh, K.N. 1966 "Spatial Pattern of Central Place in the Middle Ganga Valley", *N.G.J.I.* Vol. 12 (4), p. 43-50.

(xxiii) Nath, V. 1961 "Planning for Urban Growth" *Ind. Jour. of Social Work*, Vol. 37, pp. 119-38.

(xxiv) Bose, Ashish 1968 Urban Characteristics of Towns in India-A Statistical Analysis", *The Industrial Journal of Public Administration*, Vol. 14, pp. 457-64.

(xxv) Bose, Ashish 1972 "The Role of Small Towns in Urbanisation Process of India and Pakistan" in Readings in Micro-level Planning and Rural Growth Centres (ed.) L.K. Sen, N.I.C.D. Hyderabad.

(xxvi) Das, K.K.L. 1979 "Trends of Urbanisation in Central Mithila, Bihar, *Main Stream*.

(xxvii) Thakur, B. 1968 "Evolution of Townscape of Darbhanga" *Jour. Bih. Res. Soci.* Vol. 54 (14), pp. 345-58.

(xxviii) Tiwari, P.S. 1968 "Functional Pattern of Town in Madhya Pradesh, *N.G.J.I.*, Vol. 14 (i), pp. 41-54.

(xxix) Karimi, S.M. 1970-71 "Trends of Modern Urban Growth in Bihar Plain", *Geog. outlook*, Vol. 7, pp. 45-55.

(xxx) Sen, L.K. 1971 "Planning for Rural Growth Centres for integrated area Development : A Case Study in Miryalguda Taluka, N.I.C.D., Hyderabad, pp. 80-96.

(xxxi) Mishra, B. 1972 "Application of Growth Pole Concept to the Development of National Capital Region", *Urban and Rural Planning Thought*, Vol. 15 (2), pp. 84-108.

(xxxii) Gupta, S.K. 1975-76 "Economic Aspects of Urbanisation", Ind. Journal. Soc. Work, Vol. 36 (3-4), pp. 263-80.

(xxxiii) Sinha, V.N.P. and 1974 Hierarchy of Trade Towns in Bihar", *Ind. Geog. Studies*, Res. Bulletin No. 3, pp. 77-82.

(xxxiv) Mishra, R.P. Mahadev, P.D. and Jayashankar, D.C. (Eds) 1972 Urban Systems and Rural Development, Part I & II IDS, Mysore.

33. Sharma, N. 1989 op. cit., p. 179.

34. Das, K.K.L. 1982 "Alluvial Morphology of the North Bihar Plain : A Study in Applied Geomorphology' in perspectives in Geomorphology, Vol. Three (ed) H. S. Sharma, Concept Publishing Co. New Delhi, pp. 85-105.

35. Krishan, Gopal 1979 "Non Agricultural Workers in India", *Population Geography* Vol. 1, Nos. 1 & 2, p. 20.

36. Ganguli, Birendranath 1938 "Trends of Agriculture and Population in the Ganges Valley: A Study in Agriculture Statistics", Methuen, London.

37. Govt. of Bihar 1993 Bihar Through Figures" 1991, Directorate of Statistics and Evaluation, Patna, pp. 88-114.

38. Ahmed, E. 1979 "Geomorphology and Communication", Lecture Delivered at the All India Summer Institute of Rural Development in Applied Geography, University of Rajasthan, Jaipur, pp. 6-8.

39. Govt. of Bihar 1985 Industrial Directory of Bihar, (Third Revised Edition) Published by Bihar Small Industries Corporation, Udyog Bhawan, Patna.

Chapter-II

Urbanisation : A Contemporary Regional Perspectives

Urbanisation : An Explanation:

Urban and **Urbanisation** have recently received considerable deliberations in the academic field. These two terms 'Urban' and 'Urbanisation' signify the respective positions of scale and pace of a situation which has brought about a virtual transformation of the settlement history of population over the earth. The scale situation in this context refers to the extent of proportion of population inhabiting the form of settlement known as Urban. The pace situation refers like-wise to a tendency of transformation from one way of habitation to another. This process of transformation has come to be known as Urbanisation. Both the scale and pace phenomena of urbanisation have appeared to be a tempo-spatial event. As a tempo-spatial event, the scale and pace of Urban phenomena have moulded Urbanisation to be a temo-spatial force contribution significantly to the "Understanding of Urbanisation"[1]. The term is related to the core concern of Urban Geography. It stands for the study of Urban Concentration and Urban phenomena. By Urban Concentration what is meant in the different forms of Urban setting; and by Urban phenomena we mean all those processes that contribute to the development of Urban centres and their resultant factors. Thus the scope of the term is certainly comprehensive.

It includes the study on how cities grew and developed through ages and regions, how and when urbanisation rose to what level and what is at present and will be in future the level of urbanisation. Besides the traditional stages of concentration, centralisation, decentralisation, succession and invasion, it also includes the proper treatment of the role of "Urban implosion and explosion which has recently been inhanced"[2].

Urban development concerns the study of the phenomena of the concentration of people, that is the size of cities, which shares the common geographical basis with the rise of civilization itself [3]. The recently gained progressive changes in the role, scope and forms of urban centres have given rise to a number to a number of well known "**Urban typologies which are based on their changing salient features**". The swelling proportion of urban dwellers, witnessed at the first stage with the association of "Agricultural Revolution"; reached a new and remarkable dimension at the stage of its association with "**Industrial Revolution**".

Urban Development of North Bihar Plain : Some Distinctiveness:

The North Bihar Plain inherits a long urban past, but a short urban history. References of Vaishali, Champaran, etc., as urban centres in ancient literature indicate the long history of Urbanisation. However, the details about the degree of urbanisation a century ago have seldom been found. It is perhaps the least 'urbanised', 'least industrialised' and least developed region of the country. The degree of urbanisation in this region is not as impressive as the total population of the region.

The number of urbanites to the tune of 29.1 lakh, forming a percentage of 7.22 to total population of the region, is just half of the state's urban percentage of 13.14. The low level of urbanisation may further be taken note of in respect of the total urban population of Bihar State which is only half of the national urban percentage of 25.65. There are, on the other hand, the remaining geographical regions, viz. South Bihar Plain (15.72%) and Chotanagpur or Highland Bihar (21.45%) which exceed the state's urban proportion respectively. Of the 42 districts of the state and 20 districts of the region under study, a short fact summary of the distinctiveness of urbanisation is evident from table 2.1 (A and B).

The another feature of distinctiveness of the region is in the spatial unevenness of urban growth. An analysis of the growth behaviour of urban population of Bihar with reference to the rate of increase during 1921-91 in relation with different regional and sub-regional units holds relevance in providing a broad understanding of states Urban growth.

Urban Development of North Bihar Plain: Growth Pattern:- The growth process of urban development in the perspective of time and area, being related essentially to the study of urbanisation must follow some valid assumption.

The assumptions was worked out in the present context, Include:

Table 2.1 (A)

Urbanisation In North Bihar Plain : A Short Fact summary 1981.

Sl. No.	District Region	Level of Urbani-Sation %	Rank (State level)	Rank (Regional Level)	L.Q (State Level)	L.Q (Regional Level
1.	Saran	8.13	16	4	0.65	1.30
2.	Siwan	4.14	28	12	0.35	0.70
3.	Gopalganj	4.99	26	10	0.40	0.80
4.	West Champaran	7.34	19	7	0.59	1.18
5.	East Champaran	4.65	27	11	0.37	0.75
6.	Sitamarhi	8.62	29	13	0.36	0.72
7.	Vaishali	6.48	23	8	0.52	1.05
8.	Muzaffarpur	8.07	17	5	0.65	1.30
9.	Begusarai	10.57	12	1	0.85	1.75
10.	Samastipur	4.16	30	14	0.33	0.66
11.	Darbhanga	8.78	15	3	0.70	1.40
12.	Madhubani	3.13	31	15	0.25	0.50
13.	Saharsa	5.72	24	9	0.45	0.90
14.	Purnia	7.97	18	6	0.64	1.28
15.	Katihar	9.42	14	2	0.75	1.50
	North Bihar Plain	6.28	3	-	0.50	-
	South Bihar Plain	14.59	2	-	1.17	-
	Highland Bihar	20.80	1	-	1.67	-
	Bihar	12.49	-	-	-	-

Source: Calculated From Census of India 1981 : Series -4 Bihar, Part-II-A, General Population Tables:

Table 2.1 (B)

Urbanisation In North Bihar Plain: A Short Fact Summary, 1991

Sl. No.	District/ Region	Level of Urbani-Sation %	Rank (State level)	Rank (Regional Level)	L.Q (State Level)	L.Q (Regional Level
1.	Saran	9.10	20	7	0.69	1.26
2.	Siwan	5.29	37	18	0.40	0.73
3.	Gopalganj	5.68	34	16	0.43	0.78
4.	Paschim Champaran	10.00	16	3	0.76	1.38
5.	Purbi Champaran	5.69	33	15	0.43	0.78
6.	Sitamarhi	5.58	35	17	0.42	0.77
7.	Muzaffarpur	9.31	19	6	0.70	1.28
8.	Vaishali	6.67	27	11	0.50	0.92
9.	Begusarai	9.81	17	4	0.74	1.35
10.	Samastipur	4.96	38	19	0.37	0.68
11.	Darbhanga	8.69	21	8	0.66	1.20
12.	Madhubani	3.62	41	20	0.28	0.50

13.	Khagaria	5.95	32	14	0.45	0.82
14.	Saharsa	6.93	26	10	0.52	0.95
15.	Madhepura	6.56	28	12	0.49	0.90
16.	Purnia	8.41	22	9	0.64	1.16
17.	Katihar	9.40	18	5	0.71	1.30
18.	Araria	6.34	29	13	0.48	0.87
19.	Kishanganj	10.08	15	2	0.76	1.38
20.	Bhagalpur (Part)	16.97	11	1	1.29	2.35
	North Bihar Plain	7.22	3	-	0.55	-
	South Bihar Plain	15.72	2	-	1.63	-
	Highland	21.44	1	-	1.63	-
	Bihar	13.14	-	-	-	-

Source: Calculated from Census of India (1991) : Bihar, Population figures at a glance, Patna.

Table 2.2

Bihar : Region wise Pace of Urbanisation, 1921-91

State/Region	60 Years variation (1921-81) in per cent	District (old)	Percentage growth rate 1971-81	1981-91
North Bihar Plain	523.73.	Saran (405.2) Champaran (575.46) Muzaffarpur (442.49) Darbhanga 263.26 Purnia (911.58) Saharsa (267.09)*	49.51	39.47
South Bihar Plain	424.27	Patna (512.2) Gaya (381.4) Munger (451) (381.4) Bhagalpur (308.4)	55.51	28.06
Highland Bihar	1361.18	Dhanbad (8810.6) Hazaribagh (1208.0) Ranchi (1135.5) Singhbhum (1131.8) Palamu (455.9) Santhal (505.7) Pargana		29.86
Bihar	646.10	-	54.76	31.56

Source : Calculated from census of India, Series-4 (Bihar) Part -I; General/Final population Tables of 1961-81 and 1991

*Refers to 30 years variation (1961-91) as before 1961 the district of Saharsa was not urbanised.

1. In any study of urbanisation due importance must be attached to the study of the growth-processes which first generate and subsequently maintain or alter the scale proportions.

2 The urban growth processes are reflected in different moods of pace behaviour, viz. the proportion of people living in urban centres/ areas and the member of urban centres/areas seen in time and space perspectives.

3. The pace behaviour may suggest either a unicentral pattern at a macrospic scale, i.e. a pattern with "one major core area of higher growth and penumbral outer area with lower growth"[5], or a spatial pattern reflecting discrete regions with discrete growth rates.

4. In regional perspective the urban pace behaviour remains a dependent phenomenon to behave in response with the historical, economic, social and political situation with reference to above context, it seems imperative to look for a starting point of reference in tracing the pace behaviour of growth processes and patterns of urbanisation. Let us take the year 1921 as a base year to mark the beginning of a steady and accelerating growth in urban population well as the total population for almost all the districts of Bihar.

Although, the salient features of the pre 1921 census decades particularly since 1901 has also been included in present context at some relevant places to provide a comparative vision, in general it has been avoided because the period was featured by a deplorably low and in most cases negative growth, undoubtedly a feature of general population history. The period between 1921 and 1991 may be analysed with reference to three convenient temporal phases, each consisting of a span of two decades. These temporal phases represent also three histo-political conditions coinciding with:

i) Pre-independence upsurge,
ii) Earlyperiod of post independence planning and
iii) Contemporary post independence planned developmental action in Indian context.

An examination of the urban growth pattern of North Bihar Plain at district level yields some important observations in relation to state level urban growth;

1. The first phase constituting the decade variations of 1921-31 and 1931-41 exhibits a low to modest pace of urbanisation. Except Purnia and part of Munger district all the districts of North Bihar have shown their urban decadal growth below 25 per cent.
2. Successive phases reflect a tendency of acceleration of pace in which all the urbanised districts except Darbhanga and Saran (in 1951-61) have reached the pace mark between 25 to 50 per cent. Champaran district in the decade 1941-51and Purnia district in the decade 1951-61 have shown relatively higher urban growth ranging between 50-75 per cent.
3. It goes without saying that before 1961 the district of Saharsa was not urbanised.
4. In the next phase consisting the decade variation of 1961-71 and 1971-81 exhibits a different picture. During the decade 1961-71 Saharsa district has shown highest decadal variation, i.e. above 50 per cent due to recent growth of urban centres and maintained its pace during successive decade also. All the districts except Saran and Darbhanga in 1961-71 and West Champaran in 1971-81 have shown an average higher decadal growth ranging between 20-50 per cent and 50-75 per cent during the decade respectively.

   However, Gopalganj district has reached the pace mark of above 125 per cent in the decade of 1971-81 due to creation of new district headquarters and consequent upon it development of other urban activities.
5. During the last decade of 1981-91, population of the region increased by only 39.47 percent. The low percentage figure and the slackening of growth rates in all the macro regions of the state may be attributed to : (i) growing large scale male excessive labour migration from the countryside and urban centres in the region towards Punjab-Haryana and Delhi metropolitan areas, (ii) lack of employment opportunities and infrastructural facilities in existing urban centres did not create congenial atmosphere for attracting large scale flow of people, (iii) recurrent closure of various mining and industrial centres in the Highland Bihar, growing social tension and law and order problems in the south Bihar Plain and monotonous and stagnant economic

health of the region under study have further retarded growth pace of urbanisation.

6. In general the dynamics of state's urban population growth expresses eventful behaviour in tendencies of steadiness and spatial decentralisation. Majority of districts of North Bihar Plain record a pace mark exceeding the state's average of 31.56 per cent during 1981-91. The organisation of district units involving addition or omission of parts of parent district to create new ones, the general trend of decentralisation of developmental measures and associated results and the ground gaining fascination for urban life have set such eventful behavioural tendencies of deviations.

The spatio-temporal pace behaviour of urbanisation has not remained a self contained phenomenon. It has influenced the pace of urbanisation both in the perspective of time and area. With the gradual pace of urbanisation, the North Bihar Plain has reached a mark of a little over 7 percent level of urbanisation in 1991. The recent trends of urban growth reveal that the region will reach the mark of about 10 per cent urban scale by the close of the present century.

Urban Development of North Bihar Plain: Distribution Patterns

It appears evident that in temporal term "Urbanisation on any scale is essentially recent"[6]. The urban scale becomes, in this sense, a contemporary phenomenon of spatial system. Any geographic study in spatial system is concerned not more with any other aspects than with the "distribution of things"[7]. The contemporary assessment of the distribution pattern of urbanisation in North Bihar Plain is attempted with this conviction. Table 2.1 reveals in distribution pattern in spatial perspectives.

At first instance the distribution pattern shows that the region is least urbanised in comparison to other macro regions of the state i.e. South Bihar Plain and Highland Bihar. In relation to general urban scale of state (13.4 per cent) this region is far behind with only 7.22 per cent of urban population where as the south Bihar plain and Highland Bihar with their respective scales of 15.72 per cent and 21.44 per cent are far ahead. The ordained physio-economic destiny favouring Highland part of the state to excel the plain counter part whereas the south is more urbanised than the North Plain due

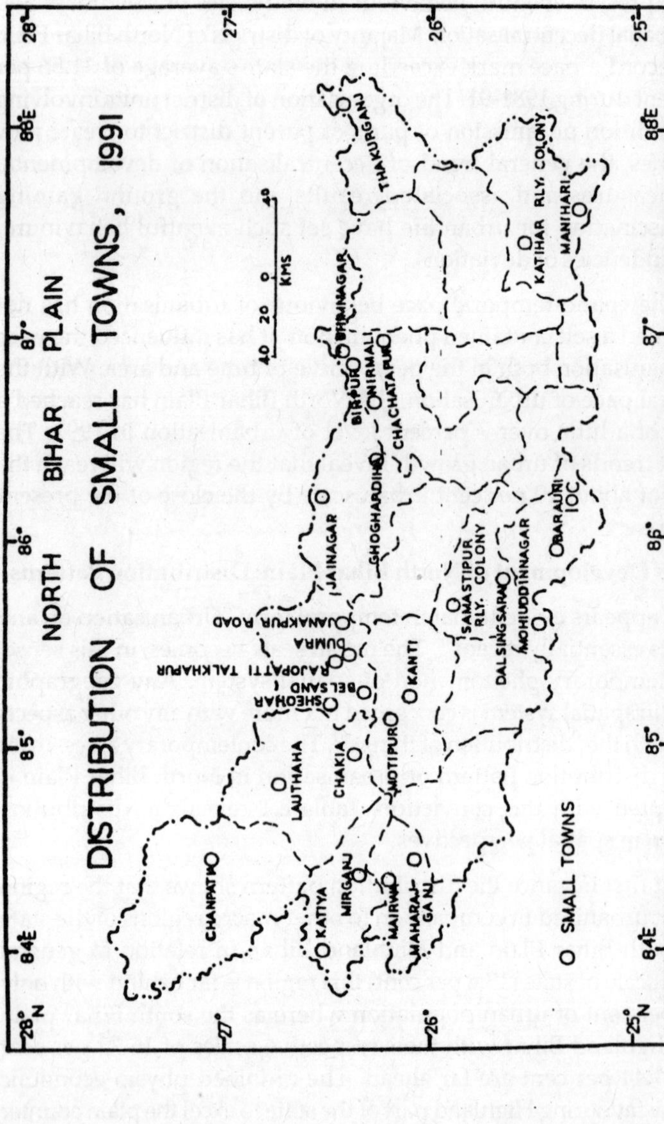

Fig. 3 Distribution of Small Towns, 1991

to old urban history, nearness to highland part, improved agricultural activities and location of state capital, etc.

The spatial variations at district level is also not very sharp in this region. The variation ranges between a high of 16.97 per cent for Naugachia sub-division (Bhagalpur) and a low of 3.62 per cent for Madhubani district. Kishanganj, Begusarai, Muzaffarpur and Katihar are relatively more urbanised (over 9 per cent) districts due to newly emerged Barauni industrial complex and railway divisional office respectively.

The overall distribution pattern is random. Among the 20 districts of the region, 9 districts including Begusarai, Katihar, Darbhanga, Vaishali, Muzaffarpur, Paschim Champaran, Purnia, Kishanganj and Saran claim a greater share in urban scale of the region exceeding location quotient of 1,00. None of the district have less than 0.5 of the location quotient or more than 2.5. It means the general feature of localized concentration of urbanisation is not apparent in this region.

The region presents, in general, a low to very low level of urbanisation at all regional scales.

Urban Development of North Bihar Plain: Sectoral Distribution of Work Force

Sectoral distribution of work force decides the quality of working population. "Participation of workers in different economic activities bears definite implication on the level of development of a region". [8] The transformation of any economy or region from the state of under development to one of developing and developed states necessarily "involves some form of change in their sectoral composition".[9] One of the important indicators of development is said to be the growth of the secondary and tertiary sectors of any economy of region.

In general the economic structure of the region is more rural and agrarian than that of the state and country as a whole.

The sectoral distribution of workers in North Bihar Plain is predominantly primary sector based. The division of work force between the two main categories viz. Agricultural Sector (Cultivator and agricultural labourers) and non-agricultural sector (other than cultivator and Agricultural labourers) have been chosen for the discussion at district level variation with the help of two successive census decades of 1981 and 1991. The relevance of this purpose is to identify specific district unit more easily as well as apparently.

The table 2.3 reveals that an overwhelming majority among district rank high to very high in agricultural sector.

— That as many as 16 districts of this region have much below the mark of state average proportion of non-agricultural work force.

— That about one-third of the district have shown almost manageable half proportion of the state average proportion of non-agricultural work force in both successive decades.

Table 2.3

North Bihar Plain : Sectoral Distribution of Urban Work Force, 1991.

Sl. No.	District	Main Workers Urban	% of Urban Main Workers to total urban Population	% of Ag. workers to main workers	% of Non Ag. Workers to main workers
1.	Saran	54913	23.43	43.38	56.62
2.	Siwan	26225	22.70	22.26	77.74
3.	Gopalganj	23140	23.88	54.49	45.51
4.	Paschim Champaran	63569	27.00	46.67	53.33
5.	Purbi Champaran	43090	24.85	41.97	58.03
6.	Sitamarhi	33296	24.93	36.90	63.10
7.	Muzaffarpur	65583	23.85	18.03	81.97
8.	Vaishali	34121	23.76	45.85	54.15
9.	Begusarai	42261	23.78	37.54	62.46
10.	Samastipur	32753	24.28	28.31	71.69
11.	Darbhanga	48245	22.09	09.69	90.31
12.	Madhubani	25300	24.61	41.56	58.44
13.	Saharsa	47305	27.55	50.32	46.68
14.	Madhepura	21310	27.73	57.81	42.19
15.	Purnia	41447	26.20	37.25	62.75
16.	Katihar	41342	25.08	20.22	79.78
17.	Khagaria	14659	24.92	36.36	63.64
18.	Araria	26878	26.27	34.69	65.31
19.	Kishanganj	27161	27.35	42.49	57.51
20.	Bhagalpur (Part)	8134	26.02	55.99	44.01
	North Bihar Plain	720742	24.76	36.18	63.82
	Bihar	2794006	24.61	21.12	78.88

Source: Calculated from Census of India, 1991 : District Primary Census Abstract, NIC, Bihar State Unit, Patna.

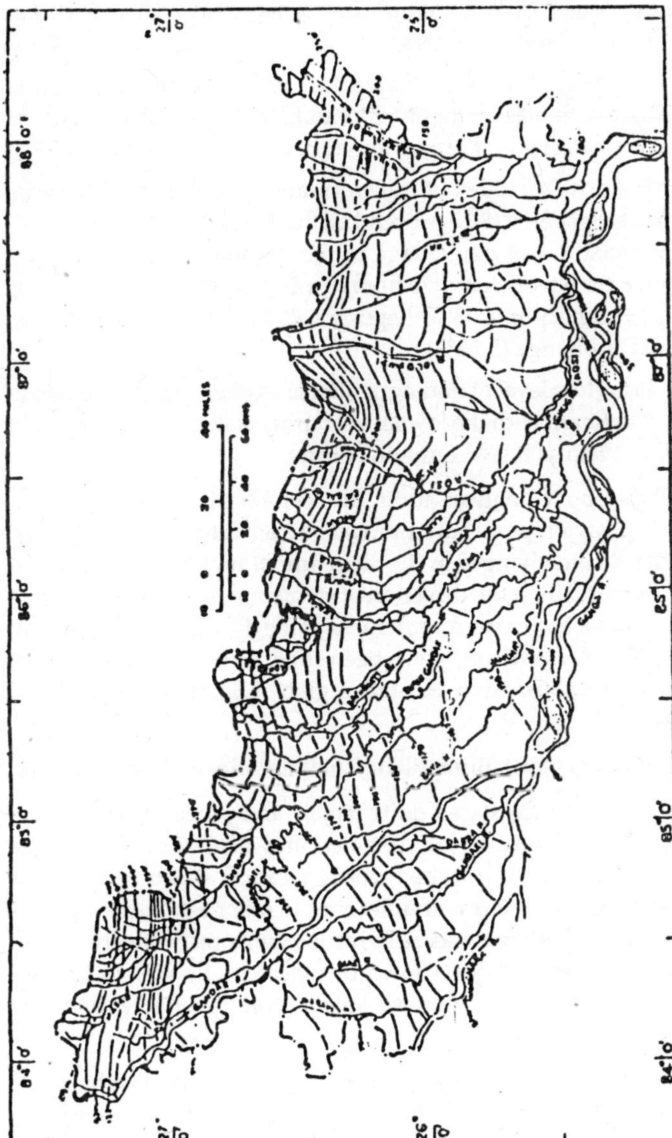

Fig. 4 North Bihar Plain-Drainage and Generalised Contours

— Although the district of North Bihar Plain have relatively very lower proportion of non-agricultural work force but they have shown+ve decadal variation during successive decades except Purnia and Katihar districts.

— That Siwan (77.74%), Muzaffarpur (81.97%), Darbhanga (90.31%), Samastipur (71.69%) and Katihar (79.78%) districts have appreciable share of non-agricultural work force in 1991.

— That a positive index of transformation is evident in the sense that except Patna (8.10 per cent) all the district which have shown appreciable +ve percentage in the decadal variation in non-agricultural work force are from North Bihar Plain. These districts are Muzaffarpur (4.33%), Begusarai (3.43%), Samastipur (3.41%) and Darbhanga (3.38%).

— That the low level of non-agricultural workers participation can be correlated with the low level of urbanisation in case of North Bihar Plain as it is a common feature.

All the above analysis about the sectoral distribution of work force and their temporal variation can be concluded as that although there have been changes in the structure of income generation in North Bihar Plain in the direction of reduction in the proportion of primary sector as per the requirement of the dynamic development, the process of restructuring has been slow, and still it is far behind the pattern established in the state region of Bihar as also of the all India level.

Small Towns of North Bihar Plain: Their Locational Characteristics

"Location can be stated quite tersely and precisely in terms of latitude and longitude, or distance and direction from other established points[10]." In other words location stated in terms of geographical ambit and with reference to other established points are known as Absolute and Relative locations respectively. Again the locational analysis of a town or place can be well judged in terms of its two different but inter-related components i.e. 'Site' and 'Situation'.

"Site embraces the precise features of terrain on which the settlement began and over which it has been spread"[11]. "Towns grow in particular places to discharge necessary functions, among which, it may be that one is of primary importance so that it may justifiably be regarded as raisin dieter of town"[12]. The precise features of terrain

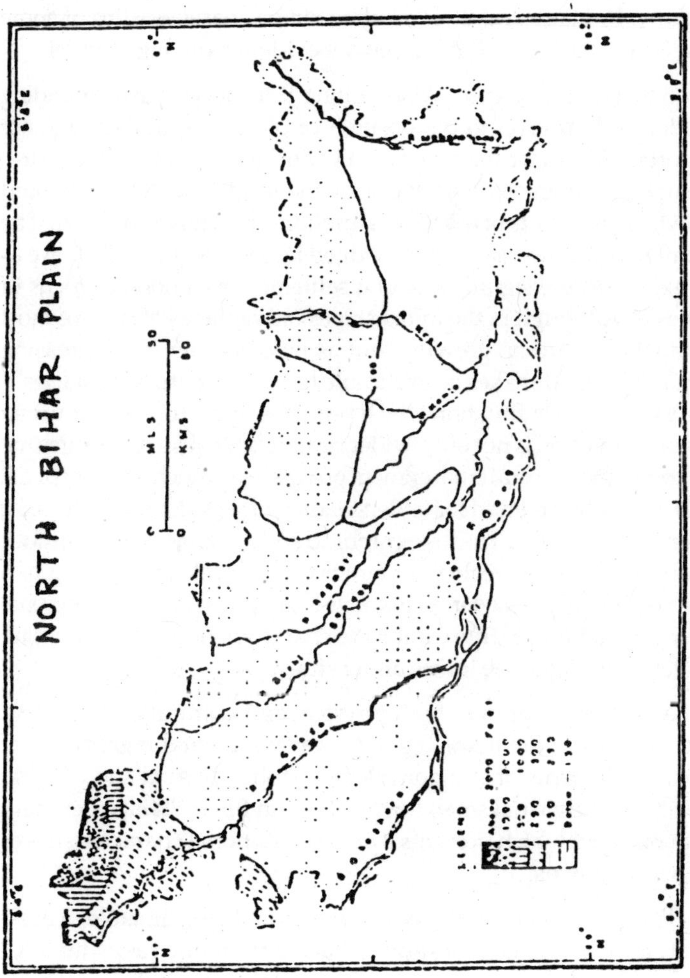

Fig. 4.1 Physical

over which the town emerges and grows refers to local physical environment. Physiography, climate, drainage etc. are the elements of physical environment and thus, they determine the 'site' characteristics of a place. Among many other impacts, the shape characteristics of small towns depends upon site. The physiography, climate, drainage and their resulted shape characteristics of some small towns of North Bihar Plain are evident from Fig. 9 and 4.

'Situation' is in a sense "Wider Setting"[13]. It refers to the surrounding relation with respect to the position of place. Naturally it is more important for the origin and growth of urban centres than the 'site'. Though all urban centres have sites, the key to their character and growth is not so much site as situation or relative location. The situation of a place may be well judged by the 'nodality' of a place as it " expresses the significance of a settlement as a node or focus of routes"[14]. Although in the initial stages "advantages of site are most stimulating to urban growth"[15] but as time goes on "the increasing demand for land makes it practicable to remove natural obstacles"[16] due to favourable situation which provides opportunities for urban growth. Situation is not only 'wider setting' but it also constitutes the economic and cultural environment of a place on much greater spatial scale. Figures as referred for understanding of sites also hold relevance in terms of situation. The topographical and geographical conditions compose the urban ecology of a region. The ecological setting of a town is, thus, expressed in terms of its local setting (site) and regional setting (situation). Figure exhibit the characteristic ecological setting of a few representative towns under study.

As a combination of both physical and cultural environment 'site' and 'situation' make the basic developmental ingredients of urban settlements of a region. Details of the physical and cultural aspects of individual small towns of North Bihar Plain are evident from **table 2.4** which presents a precise locational characteristics of individual towns:

The geo-structural, physical make up and bio-climatological set up of North Bihar Plain constitute what may be termed as its' material environment' which always influence the town development tendencies. It is due to this material environment that towns in North Bihar Plain have grown in Pari Passu with man's accomplishment in making plain Bihar as state's grainary; and emergence of centres performing tertiary occupation in pre dominance.

Table 2.4 - North Bihar Plain : Physical Aspects and Location of Small Towns, 1991

Sl. no.	Name of the Small Towns	Rainfall in c.m.	Temperature maxi	Temperature Mini.	Road distance in Kms. From State H.Q.	Distirct H.Q.	Sub.Dvn H.Q.	Nearest City	Railway Station figures in bracket refer in 10 cms. to st. distance from the Small towns.	Bus Route	Navigable River/ Canal(with in 10 Kms
1.	Mirganj	1050.40	45.00	6.00	Patna 190	Gopalganj 16	Gopalganj 16	Chapra 93	Hathwa 9	Mirganj 0	-
2.	Chanpatia	1221.80	44.80	6.10	Patna 258	Betiah 18	Betiah 18	Muzaffar pur 146	Chanpatia 0	Chanpatia	Sikrahna R
3.	Katihar Rly. Colony	1483.70	46.00	4.10	Patna 325	Katihar 0	Katihar 0	Bhagalpur 155	Katihar 0	Katihar 0	-
4.	Motipur	1213.40	41.70	5.60	Patna 135	Muzaffar pur 35	Muzaffar pur 35	Muzaffarpur 35	Motipur 0		
5.	Manihari	968.50	46.00	4.10	Patna 355	Katihar 30	Katihar 30	Katihar 30	Manihari 0	Manihari 0	Ganges R
6.	Maharajganj	111.52	38.20	6.20	Patna 110	Siwan 22	Siwan 22	Chapra 45	Maharajganj 0	Maharajganj 0	- -
7.	Jainagar	1197.60	43.30	4.00	Patna 265	Madhu-bani 32	Madhu-bani 32	Darbh-anga 54	Jainagar 0	Jainagar 0	Kamla R
8.	Chchatapur	1832.00	44.90	4.00	Patna 285	Saharsa 50	Birpur 21	Saharsa 50	Raghopur 36	Cgcgataoyr 0	Kosi R
9.	Dalsing Sarai	1250.00	42.80	6.40	Patna 166	Samasti pur 24	Samasti pur 24	Darbh-anga 70	Dalsing-Sarai 0	Dalsing Sarai 0	Kamala R
10.	Mairwa	945.10	40.00	5.00	Patna 189	Siwan 21	Siwan 21	Chapra 93	Mairwa 0	Mairwa 0	-
11.	Birpur	18323.00	44.90	7.40	Patna 305	Saharsa 90	Birpur 0	Bhagalpur 160	Bathnaha 32	Birpur 0	Kosi R

12.	Kanti	1213.40	41.70	5.60	Patna 120	Muzaffar pur 12	Muzaffar pur 12	Muzaffar pur 12	Kanti 0	Kanti 0	-
13.	Belsand	1064.00	45.20	5.20	Patna 124	Sitamarhi 2	Sitamarhi 20	Muzaffar pur 44	Muzaffar pur 20	Belsand 0	Bagmati R
14.	Sheohar	1064.00	45.20	5.20	Patna 146	Sitamarhi 36	Sitamarhi 36	Muzaffar pur 64	Sitamarhi 36	Sheohar	Bagmati R
15.	Nirmali	1267.80	42.90	5.50	Patna 310	Saharsa 80	Birpur 50	Darbh-anga 71	Nirmali 0	Nirmali 0	Kosi R
16.	Thakurganj	2112.00	41.40	4.00	Patna 414	Purnea 124	Kishan-ganj 57	Siliguri 48	Thakur-ganj 0	Thakur-ganj 0	-
17.	Chakia	1094.20	41.00	5.20	Patna 612	Motihari 32	Motihari 32	Muzaffar pur 48	Chakia 0	Chakia 0	
18.	Kataiya	1050.40	45.00	6.00	Patna 215	Gopal-ganj 38	Gopal-ganj 38	Gorakh-pur 48	Hatwa 18	Kataiya 0	-
19.	Barauni I.O.C.	1165.80	43.80	7.60	Patna 165	Begu-Sarai 2	Begu-Sarai 2	Munghyr 39	Begu-Sarai 2	Barauni	Ganga R
20.	Ghoghardiha	1263.80	42.90	5.50	Patna 148	Madhu-bani 60	Jhanjhar-pur 36	Darbh-anga 88	Ghoghar-0	Ghoghar-0	Bhutahi Balan R
21.	Dumra	1064.00	45.20	5.20	Patna 166	Sitamarhi 4	Sitamarhi 4	Muzaffar-pur 55	Sitamarhi 4	Dumra 0	Lakhandei R
22.	Samastipur Rly. Colony	1250.00	42.80	6.40	Patna 191	Samasti-pur 0	Samasti-pur 0	Darbh-anga 40	Samasti-pur 0	Samasti-pur 0	Burhi Gandak R
23.	Mohiuddin-Nagar	1160.00	41.00	6.00	Patna 176	Samasti-pur 55	Samasti-pur 55	Muzaffar-pur 110	Mohiuddin-Nagar 0	Mohiddin-Nagar	Ganges R
24.	Rajopatti Talkha-pur Dumara	1064.00	45.20	5.20	Patna 160	Sitamarhi 3	Sitamarhi 3	Muzaffar-pur 53	Sitamarhi 3	Rajopatti 0	
25.	Janakpur Rd.	1100.00	42.50	3.50	Patna 166	Sitamarhi 34	Sitamarhi 34	Darbhanga 65	JanakpurRd. 0	Janakpur Rd. 0	-
26.	Lauthaha	1210.80	41.60	4.90	Patna 190	Motihari 1	Motihari 1	Muzaffar-pur 76	Motihari Court 0	Lauthaha 0	Dhamanti R
27.	Bhimnagar	1832.00	44.90	7.40	Patna 300	Saharsa 85	Birpur 5	Bhagalpur 155	Raghopur 40	Bhimnagar 0	Kosi R

Source: Census of India (1981) Seires-4 Bihar: Part XA Town Directory, pp. 84-97.

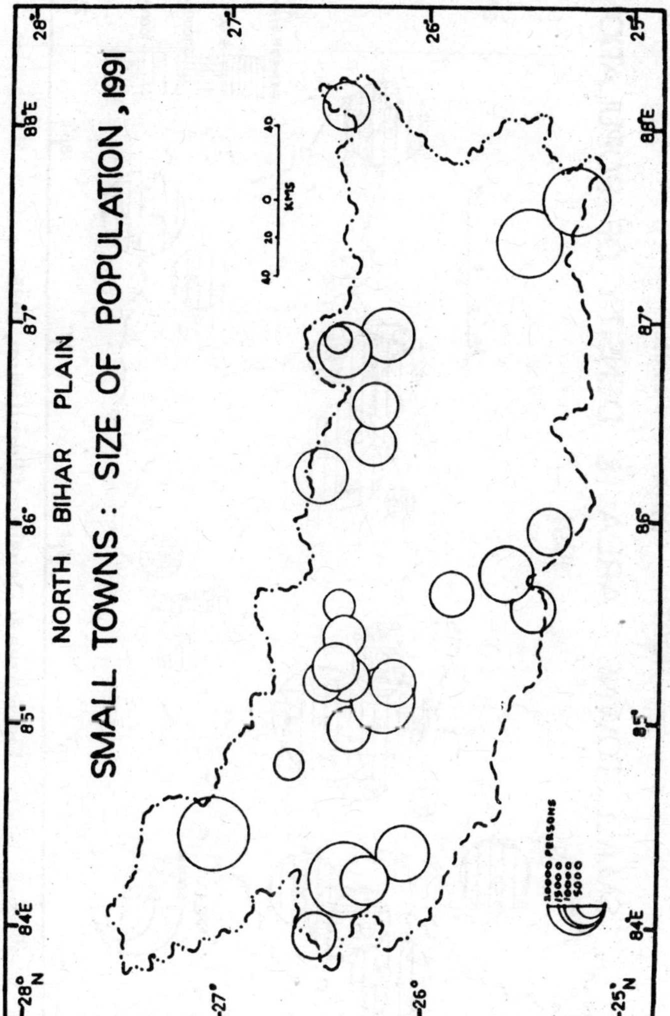

Fig. 5 Small Town: Size of population 1991

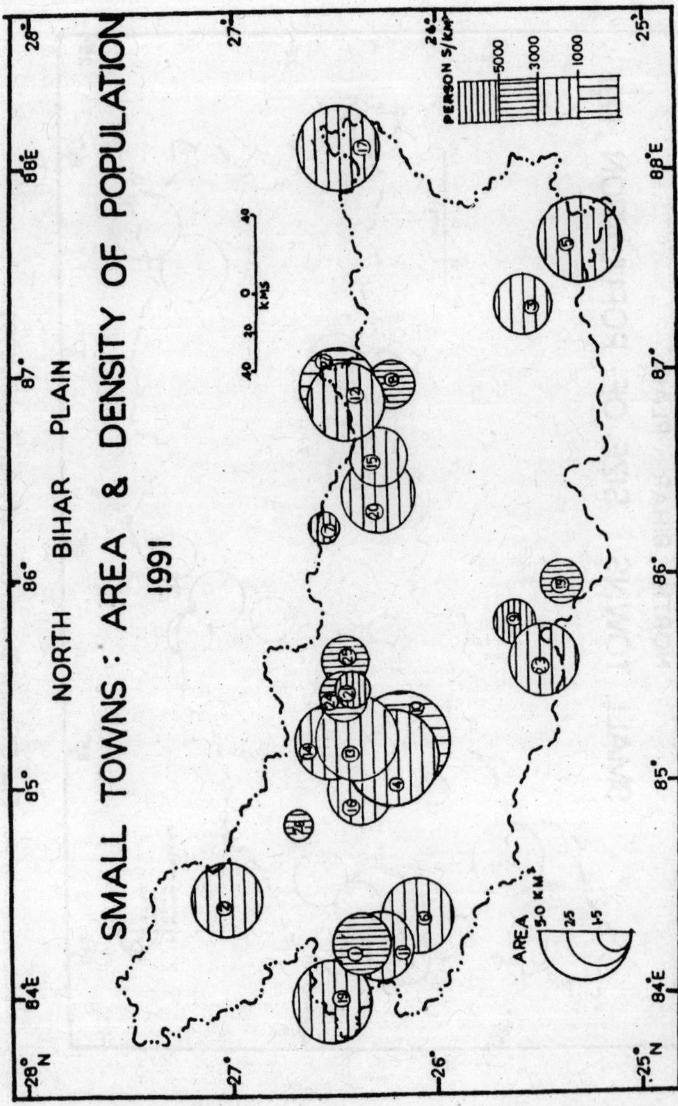

Fig. 6 Area & Density of Population, 1991

Small Towns of North Bihar Plain : Their Number, Distribution and Density

Deeply concerned with obvious consideration of "distribution of things"[17], geography has been referred to the one that constitutes a discipline of distance. Unevenness in the distribution of things is a common phenomenon in geographical studies. Small towns of North Bihar Plain also present an uneven distribution pattern as the level of urbanisation does. The distribution pattern of small towns as evident from table 2.5 and Fig. 7 reveals :

— That there is no zone of maximum concentration.
— That the towns among river Ganga and near international boundary of Nepal from a weak linear pattern.
— That between the two linear patterns of distribution there is almost a vacant mid land.
— That about one third of total grids are lying vacant.

The following frequency table (2.5) advocates, the nature and degree of the concentration of small towns.

Table 2.5
Spatial Pattern of Small Towns, 1991

Group of Towns	F.O.	Total Number of Towns	Grid Number
5	1	5	17
4	0	0	-
3	1	3	22
2	2	4	15 and 18
1	15	15	5, 7, 9, 10, 20, 21, 22, 25, 27, 30, 39, 40, 44, 46, 51
		27	

Based on Fig. 7 F.O = Frequency of occurrences Ref. Fig. 7

Nature and degree of towns concentration over a region are best explained in terms of spacing. Spacing of small towns in North Bihar Plain at different regional scales has been worked out by using the formula :

S= A/N where A=Area of the region.
N= No. of small towns.

For this purpose the calculation has been made on the basis of old district to avoid areal gaps because some newly formed districts have

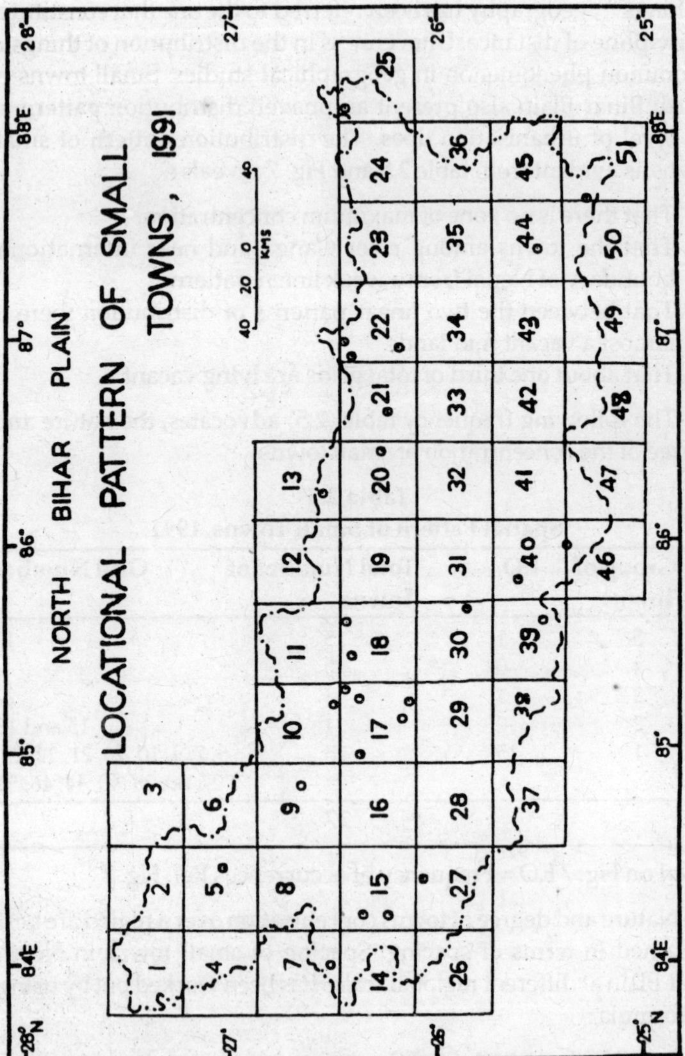

Fig. 7 Locational Pattern of small Towns, 1991

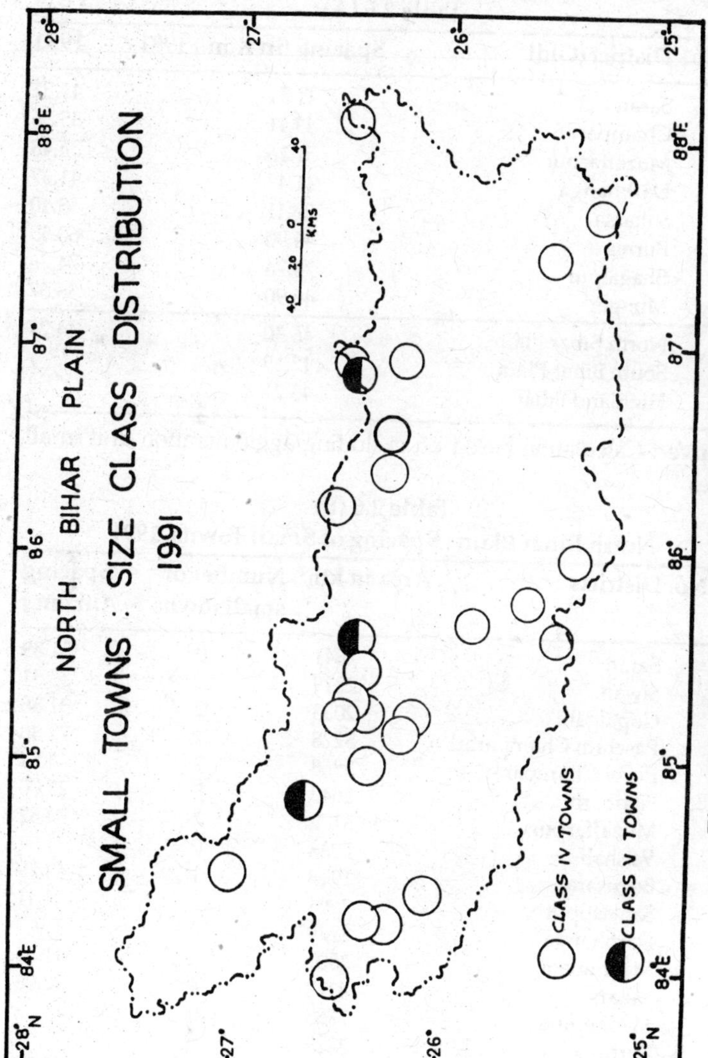

Fig. 8 Small Towns: Size Class Distribution, 1991

no small towns. Hence, the number of small towns and the area of their respective districts (Old-1971) have been included in calculation. The spacing of small towns are evident from table 2.6 A and B.

Table 2.6 (A)

Sl No.	District (Old)	Spacing (in K.m.) 1981	1991
1.	Saran	41.51	41.51
2.	Champaran	49.11	55.36
3.	Muzaffarpur	51.16	33.48
4.	Darbhanga	41.47	41.67
5.	Saharsa	38.11	38.40
6.	Purnia	46.90	60.55
7.	Bhagalpur	74.76	74.76
8.	Munger	46.90	56.67
	North Bihar Plain	46.30	44.27
	South Bihar Plain	42.19	-
	Highland Bihar	45.21	-

Source : Calculation based on excluding agglomeration unit in all cases.

Table 2.6 (B)

North Bihar Plain : Spacing of Small Towns, 1991

Sl. No.	Districts	Area in km²	Number of small towns	Spacing (in km.)
1.	Saran	2641	0	51.39
2.	Siwan	2219	2	33.31
3.	Gopalganj	2033	2	31.88
4.	Paschim Champaran	5228	1	72.30
5.	Purbi Champaran	3968	2	44.54
6.	Sitamarhi	2643	5	23.00
7.	Muzaffarpur	3172	2	39.82
8.	Vaishali	2036	0	-
9.	Begusarai	1918	1	43.79
10.	Samastipur	2904	3	31.11
11.	Darbhanga	2279	0	-
12.	Madhubani	3501	2	41.84
13.	Saharsa	4112	4	32.06
14.	Madhepura	1788	0	-
15.	Purnia	3229	0	-
16.	Katihar	3057	2	39.10
17.	Khagaria	1486	0	-
18.	Araria	2830	0	-
19.	Kishanganj	1884	1	43.40

North Bihar Plain	52928	27	44.28
Bihar	173877	-	-

Source: Calculated from census of India, 1991 : Series- 4, Bihar, **Town wise Primary Census Abstract Data,** Patna.

The above tables reveals that the spacing of small towns at district level bears appreciable ditinctiveness, not at macro-regional levels. It is noticeable that the spacing of small towns should be viewed in the relative terms of total town's spacing for a desired spatial planning which has been worked out 29.21 (1981) and 26.74 (1991) for North Bihar Plain.

It is to note that the new districts of Saran, Vaishali, Darbhanga, Madhepura, Purnia, Araria and Khagaria have no small towns to and the current gained number of 27 (Twenty seven) small towns in the region have a very recent past. There were only 3 small towns in the region around the year 1931 and they gradually multiplied to 4, 8, 14, 16, and 25 in the successive census decades of 1941, 1951, 1961, 1971 and 1981. It has increased its family with appreciable number of 25 in 1981 and 27 in the last census year of 1991.

As regards density of small towns, the average density of population (1991) of small towns in North Bihar Plain is 2,169 persons per square kilometre, but it has a wide range of variation. The density of population in small towns vary between a high of 10, 954 persons per km^2 for Jainagar to a low of 640 persons per km^2 for Bhimnagar. Density of small towns (Appendix-I) shows a perfect negative relation with area, i.e. the higher the area, the lower the density and the lower the area, the higher the density (Fig.). A rank analysis correlating the areal size and density size of small towns places 6 of them in the category high area high density category and remains a major group of small towns having high rank in area but low in density.

The correlation between population size and density size of small towns places 7 of them in the category of those with high population and high density, 7 in the category of those with low population but high density 6 in the category of thsoe with high population but low density and 5 in the category of those with low population and low density rank. This therefore, leaves ample scope of diversification of such towns. There is also another group with high density but low area presenting spatial problem of consequence. There are very few towns showing positive relation between area and population rank. Strategies for development of small towns, thus, assume justification in aiming at providing at least a near positive, if not perfectly, relation between area and population of most centres, if not for all.

Small Towns of North Bihar Plain : Size Characteristics

The size character of small towns of North Bihar Plain may be quantified in terms of '**Size Index**' and "**Urban Size Index**" obtained by the application of formula :

$$S.I = \frac{Pc \times 100}{PR}$$

Where PC =Population of Small Towns

PR =Population of Region i.e. district.

$$U.S.I. = \frac{Pc \times 100}{UPR}$$ where UPR = urban Population of Region.

Different small towns have been grouped under index categories in the name of their size rank as given in Appendix-I

Table 2.7

North Bihar Plain : Size Index of Small Towns, 1991

Sl. No.	S.I. Range	Small Towns size Rank		U.S.I. Range	Small towns Size Rank	
1.	0.00-0.50	26(0.19)	27(0.22)	0.00-10.00	22 (8.59)	25 (7.18)
		25 (0.40)	23(0.40)		27 (3.30)	26 (3.35)
		20 (0.42)	22 (0.42)		10 (5.83)	4 (6.48)
		24 (0.45)	16 (0.45)		19 (7.08)	16 (7.90)
		21 (0.48)			15 (8.02)	24 (8.06)
					23 (8.16)	2 (8.20)
					8 (9.75)	12 (8.58)
2.	0.51-1.00	10 (0.54)	15 (0.55)	10.01-20.00	5 (10.05)	14 (10.42)
		14 (0.58)	7 (0.59)		13 (10.59)	3 (11.03)
		12 (0.59)	13 (0.59)		20 (11.69)	9 (12.40)
		4 (0.60)	9 (0.61)		11 (13.17)	17 (13.68)
		8 (0.67)	19 (0.69)		18 (13.76)	6 (14.86)
		11 (0.71)	18 (0.78)		7 (16.52)	
		6 (0.79)	2 (0.82)			
		5 (0.94)				
3	1.01-1.50	3 (1.03)	1 (1.15)	20.01-30.00	1 (20.33)	
		17 (1.38)				

Number refer to size rank of small towns as in Appendix-I.

It becomes clear from table 2.7 that majority of small towns appears well in low to very low '**Size Index**' and only a few with appreciable indices and that also due only to absence of big cities in corresponding district. This asks for strategies for development of these towns so as to provide a viable Urban system in the region.

The slow growth of small towns and the stagnation, decay and declassification of several such towns in a period of accelerated urbanisation is a phenomenon which has not received adequate attention from demorgraphers and other social scientists.

A rank analysis correlating the population size and areal size of small towns places 6 of them in the category of those with high population and high area, 7 in the category of those with high population and low area, 7 in the category of those with high area and low population and remaining 5 in the category of those with low population and low area.

Small Towns of North Bihar Plain: A Probe into Regional Development

The least urbanised, least industrialised and least developed region of North Bihar Plain needs an overall economic planning. The rural and urban planning may be very fruitful in the planning of resource based- planning of small town because these centres exist between the mid point of two forms of settlement. The region's economy may be treated as backward, stagnant, over populated, traditional and mainly agricultural. The existing small towns provide a new life to the regions economic personality if they are planned as centres of development. The planning perspectives of these towns require the examinations of their possibility, limitations, resource orientation and other developmental potentialities in terms of regional and sub-regional planning levels.

In the inaugural session of two-day workshop on Integrated Development of small and Medium Towns as strategy for urban development in Bihar (1989), the Development commissioner Mr. S. Saran emphasized the necessity of reorganising the system of human settlement in the context of the whole country and also the need for encouraging the small and medium towns to play an active part in rural and metropolitan development. He stressed that integrated development of small and medium towns is the appropriate strategy to check the alarming growth of population and increasing

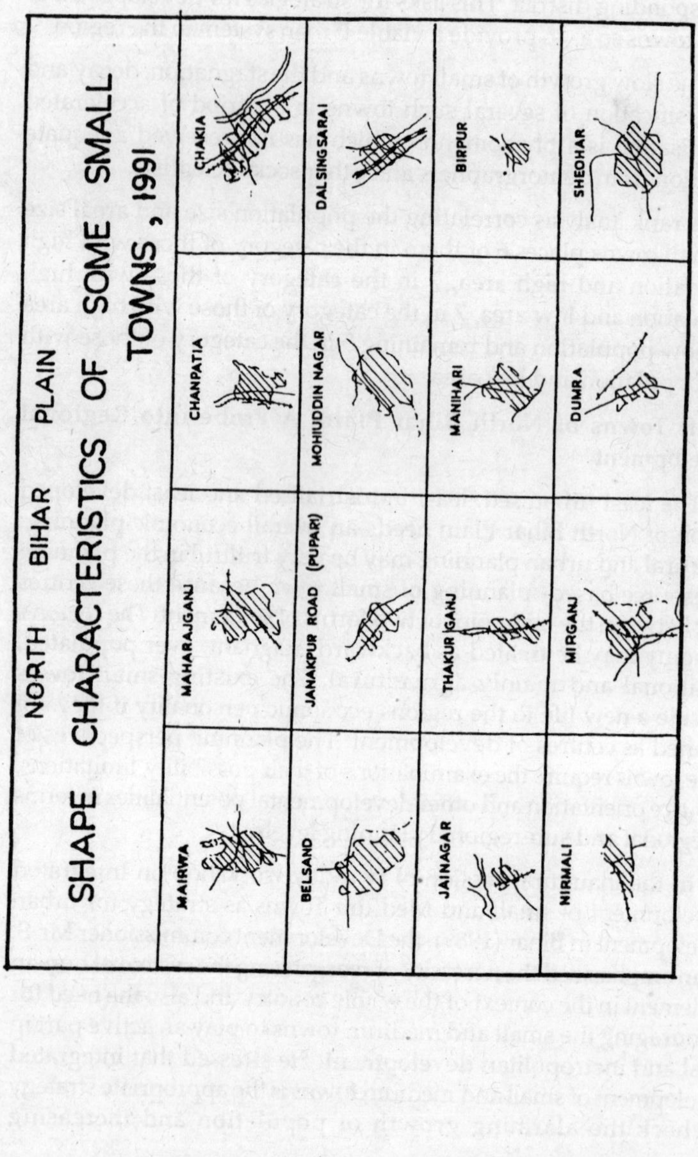
NORTH BIHAR PLAIN
SHAPE CHARACTERISTICS OF SOME SMALL TOWNS, 1991
MAIRWA
MAHARAJGANJ
CHANPATIA
CHAKIA
BELSAND
JANAKPUR ROAD (PUPARI)
MOHIUDDIN NAGAR
DALSINGSARAI
JAINAGAR
THAKUR GANJ
MANIHARI
BIRPUR
NIRMALI
MIRGANJ
DUMRA
SHEOHAR

Fig. 9

concentration of people in urban areas. For the result oriented implementation of urban development programme specific recommendations and time bound action will help in integrated development of small towns of the region.

The emergence and the sustained growth of small towns have the scope to create a viable settlement hierarchy to facilitate rural-urban continuum. This would remove the existing gap between large towns and small rural settlement. For this purpose the different levels of planning unit, have to be viewed' as a magnified shape of a metropolis where in its residents live in various localities and avail themselves of facilities at the nearest market place but also traverse long distances for next higher order facilities, if they are not available at the nearest market place and so on"[18]. "With the growing habitat-concern now it has been advocated that small towns might be treated growth centres especially in developing world"[19]. It has been highlighted that small towns have the potentially capacity to "utilize rural man power and elicit human creativity"[20]. So they should be treated as **'Investment Cluster'**. It has been rightly remarked that the main concern of the policy makers in the developing world, of which the region under study is a part, is economic progress. For operationalization of this structure the policy makers and planners must conceive small towns "as an instrument for quickening the rate of growth, development and transformation"[21]. It is possible only through the proper spatial integration between small towns and the surrounding rural territory. The strategy for the development of small towns in North Bihar Plain reveals its justification in the more sensitive sense:

— That here exist an appreciable hierarchical imbalance among human- habitat system in which these urban centres may be treated as worst sufferer.

— That resource utilization at local level are far away from satisfactory level. Either they are unutilised or exploited by big urban centres.

— That as an optimum unit of regional planning scale, widely spread small towns provide suitable place for the developmental action because big urban centres create only centralized development at one hand while villages present more difficulty with their vast number.

— That transformation of unisectoral economic system to a desired level is only possible through these centres in the sense that they may cater to the needs of people with immediate effect.

The role of small towns in district planning context is also notable because they may facilitate the action of development as points of connection between district headquarters and rural hinterlands. Ultimately, instead of treating urbanisation as a process of working against rural development, the attempt treat urbanisation as means to develop rural areas. The implicit assumption behind this approach is that image of the society in the future.

References Cited in the Text:

1. Breese, G. 1969 **'Urbanisation in Newly Developing Countries'**, Prentice Hall of India, Pvt. Ltd., New Delhi, p. 12
2. Sharma, N. 1980 'Temporal Dimensions of Urban Geography" in Recent Trends and Concept in Geography, (ed) R.B. Mandal and V.N. P. Sinha, Concept Publishing Co. New Delhi, p. 113
3. Smailes, E. 1953 **'Geography of Towns'** Hutehinson University Library, London, p.7
4. Robson, B.T. 1973 **'Urban Growth** : Approach', **Methuen & Co. Ltd.** London, p. 4
5. Ibid, p. 111
6. Carter, H. 1982 **'The Study of Urban Geography'**, Edward Arnold, p. 23
7. Aurousean, M. 1924 Recent Contribution in Urban Geography '*Geographical Review*' Vol. XIV, No. 3, p. 445
8. Sharma, N. 1977 "Strategies for Development of Medium size Towns in Bihar" : A Study in Development Technology ; Ph. D. Thesis, Bhagalpur University, p. 54
9. Guru, D.D. 1987 **An Analysis of Changes in Sectoral Composition State Domestic Products of Bihar, 'Bihar : Stagnation of Growth**, (ed) A. N. Sharma & S. Gupta, Patna, p. 28
10. Smailes, A.E. 1953 '**Op. Cit**', p. 41
11. Dickinson, R.E. 1967 '**The Scope and Status of Urban Geography : Rou Hedge and Kegal Paul,** Ltd. London, p. 12
12. Smailes, A.E. 1953 '**Op. Cit.**' p. 41

13. Idem p. 42

14. Dickinson, R.E. 1967 '**Op. Cit**', p. 21

15. Smailes, A.E. 1953 '**Op. Cit**', p 53

16. Doran, H.P. and Hinman, A.G. 1928 '**Urban Land Economics**, New York, p. 28

17. Auroussean, M. 1924 '**Op.cit.**' p. 445

18. Mishra, G.K. 1969 **The Role of Small Towns in District Planning : A Case of Raichur District**, Place of small Towns in India, (ed.) R. L. Singh & Rana, P.B. Singh, N.G.S.I., Varanasi, p. 210

19. U.N.O.1978 '**The Significance of Rural Housing in Integrated Rural Development**', ST/ESA/77, New York, p. 36

20. Johnson, E.A.J. 1972 '**The Integration of Agrarian, Commercial and Industrial Activities in Functional Economic Areas in NCAER**, p. 70

21. Ibid, p. 71

Chapter-III
Growth Behaviour of Small Towns

Growth Behaviour of Small Towns

Urban centres have proved to signify a tempo-spatial event as it has been designated as a "**point of assembly**"[1]. An urban centre emerges not to stay as it is. It tends to multiply and grow. It serves to be both a "container" and a magnet'[2]. it choses location over space. In its tempo-spatial dimension urban centres behave, therefore in a fashion that they become points of distribution. By virtue of their tendencies to multiply in number, to grow in size and to act as spatial force'[3] in varying degrees, urban centres have been experiencing peaks of growth and periods of decline affecting considerably the pace of urbanisation in time and area perspectives.

The spatio-temporal growth behaviour of urban centres depend upon their size class also. The small towns containing lower size classes of IV, V and VI categories of towns is at the bottom of hierarchy and have shown district growth behaviour. In general, small towns are slow growing urban centres in India. In particular case of Bihar, an observation reveals that "Urban centres in comparative terms produced a pace behaviour to see big cities growing continuously and rapidly, the medium size towns growing modestly but exhibiting a weakening trend of continuity and small towns growing stagnantly or even negatively'[4]. The case of small towns of North Bihar Plain follows the same trend. It is noticeable that the growth of small towns tells the tale of fluctuating fortunes and misfortunes through different decades of census and each small town has its own history of growth. To provide a detailed growth analysis, it is essential to trace the growth of individual small towns of the study area since 1901.

Growth of Individual Small Towns in the Region since 1901 :

Each census year from 1901 to 1991 bears some relevance in the temporal growth history of small towns in the region. It is noticeable at first instance that the present number of 27 small towns in North Bihar Plain is the out come of temporal addition in its family through every decade. Of the present 27 small towns only three were in 1901 census. Before analysing their growth behaviour in terms of population, it seems relevant to know their first existence in census decades since 1901 to provide in a sequence order its growth history. For this purpose, the table 3.1 serves the need.

Table 3.1
North Bihar Plain: Growth History of Individual Small Towns 1901-1991

Census year	Existing Number -Subtraction	Name of small Towns added(+) Subtracted (-)
1901	3	Lalganj, Rosera, Mirganj
1911	3+0	Lalganj, Rosera, Mirganj
1921	3+1-1	Jainagar (+), Mirganj (-)
1931	3+0	Lalganj, Rosera, Jainagar
1941	3+1	Chanpatia (+)
1951	4+4	Sugauli (+), Banmankhi Bazar (+), Murliganj (+), Maharajganj (+), Birpur (+) Nirmali (+)
1961	8+6	Jogbani (+), Banmankhi Bazar (+), Murliganj (+), Maharajganj (+), Birpur (+), Nirmali (+),
1971	14+3	Bihariganj (+), Gogri Jamalpur (+), Mairwa (+)
1981	17+8	Dighwara (+) Bahadurganj (+) Jhanjharpur (+), Manihari (+), Belsand (+), Thakurganj, Mohiuddinnagar (+) and Janakpur Road
1991	25+13-11	Katihar Rly. Colony (+) Motipur (+) Chatapur (+) Kanti (+) Seohar (+) Kataiya (+) Barauni I.O.C. (+) Ghoghardiha (+) Dumara (+) Samastipur Rly. Colony (+) Rajopatti Talkhapur Dumra (+) Lauthaha (+) Bhimnagar (+) Subtracted (moved to class III Status): Sugauli, Lalganj, Bihariganj, Gogri, Jamalpur, Rosera, Jogbani, Banmankhi, Bazar, Dighwara, Bahadurganj, Murliganj, Jhanjharpur.

Source : Census of India (1981), Series-4: Bihar Town Directory, Part XA and Town wise Primary Census Abstract 1991.

Table 3.1 reveals-That there were only 3 small towns in 1901. They were Mirganj, Lalganj and Rosera.

That except Mirganj, no towns among these 27 lost their urban status in any decade. Mirganj lost its status in 1921 and regained in 1951.

Among these three small towns Rosera has shown continuous growth except in the census decades of 1901-11 and 1911-21. Its population increased by 303.07 per cent during 1901-81. The increase is in the sense that the town had experienced negative growth rates of -24.58 per cent and -0.43 per cent during 1901-11 and 1911-21 decades respectively. It has got the status of medium size town as its size of population increased to 24, 234 in 1991. Similarly, during the period of 1901-81, the population of Lalganj increased by only 69.72 per cent. The low percentage increase is due to the fact this town had experienced a relatively high negative growth rates of -26.69 per cent and -27, 22 per cent during the period of 1901-11 and 1911-21 respectively. It also got the status of medium size town at the last census and has a population of 24, 927 in 1991. It is due to an all-round development of road transport, trade as well as visible signs of increase in the infra-structure of the economy.

After regaining the urban status in 1951 in the proceeding decades of 1961-71 and 1971-81 in Mirganj (size rank-01) the population increased by an appreciable percentage of 28.36 and 48.80 respectively. However the current decade (1981-91) has experienced a much lower growth rate of (13.61) per cent only.

Jainagar (size rank 07) emerged as a small town in 1921 and has shown flexible growth rates in proceeding decades. Its population growth rate was only 7.35 per cent during 1921-31 while in 1931-41, the town displayed a decrease in its population by the percentage of -52.83. Since 1941-51 decade the town has been on the way of continuous but slow growth. During the last decade (1981-91), however it has experienced a much higher growth rate (42.01 per cent) due to visible signs of increase in infrastructure of the economy and growing Indo-Nepal boarder trade.

No new towns emerged in the census decade of 1931 and only one small town Chanpatia (size rank-02) gets urban status in 1941. This town has shown negative growth rate of 16.28 per cent during 1961-71 decade and in the remaining decades the increase of

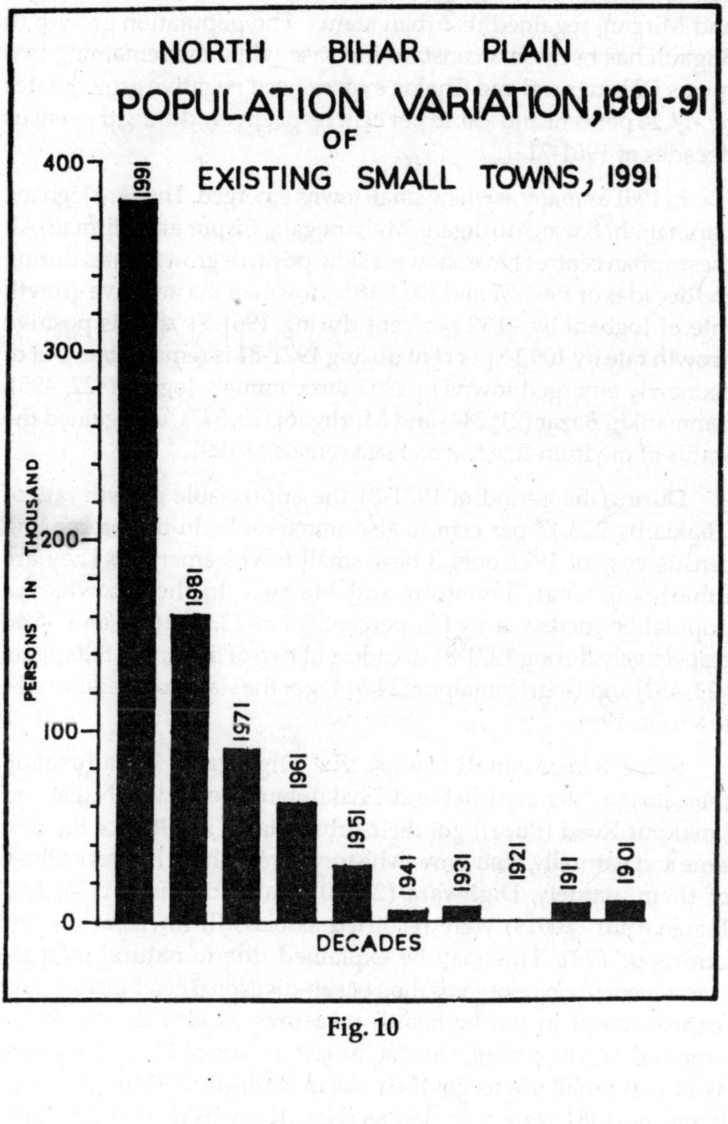
NORTH BIHAR PLAIN
POPULATION VARIATION, 1901-91
OF
EXISTING SMALL TOWNS, 1991
PERSONS IN THOUSAND
400
300
200
100
0
1991
1981
1971
1961
1951
1941
1931
1921
1911
1901
DECADES

Fig. 10

population has not been appreciable.

The temporal history of small towns reveal that the net increase in the number of small towns has been on the rise since 1951 when 4 new small towns viz. Sugauli, Dalsingsarai and Chakia emerged and Mirganj regained its urban status. The population growth of Sugauli has been on a constant increase while the remaining two towns Dalsingsarai and Chakia experienced negative growth rates by -14.28 per cent and -50.18 per cent respectively during the census decades of 1961-71.

In 1961 as many as 6 new small towns emerged. They are Jogbani, Banmankhi Bazar, Murliganj, Maharajganj, Birpur and Nirmali. All these urban centres have shown a slow positive growth rates during the decades of 1961-71 and 1971-181. However the negative growth rate of Jogbani by -0.32 per cent during 1961-71 and its positive growth rate by 109.16 per cent during 1971-81 is remarkable. Out of six newly emerged towns in 1961 three namely Jogbani (22, 495), Banmankhi Bazar (21, 244) and Murliganj (20, 547) have gained the status of medium size town in last census of 1991.

During the period of 1971-81 the appreciable growth rate of Chakia by 223.47 per cent is also remarkable. In the preceeding census year of 1971 only 3 new small towns emerged. They are Bihariganj, Gogri Jamalpur and Mairwa. In these towns the population increased by the percentage of 22.38, 16.38 and 76.46 respectively during 1971-81 decade and two of them, viz. Bihariganj (23, 452) and Gogri Jamalpur (24,614) got the status of Medium size towns in 1991.

Some 8 new small towns, viz. Dighwara, Bahadurganj, Jhanjahrpur, Manihari, Belsand, Thakurganj, Mohiuddin Nagar and Janakpur Road (Pupri) got their urban status in 1981 for the first time and naturally, their growth history is very short. However, three of them, namely, Dighwara (22650), Bahadurganj (21123) and Jhanjharpur (20019) were recorded as class-III towns at the last census of 1991. This may be explained due to natural increase consequent upon re-organisation of sub-divisional headquarters and improvement in public health measures as also due to latent economic development. During the last decade of 1981-91 as many as 13 new small towns got their urban status in 1991 and 11 small towns on 1981 were recorded as class III towns in 1991 (cf. Table 3.1). Naturally, the growth history of new small towns is not available while upgradation of 11 small towns has already been dealt with. In total, there are 27 small towns as per 1991 census in the region under study which have been ranked on the basis of their current size of population and are given in the Appendix-I.

The above growth history of individual small towns reveals the fact that no small town of this region has a constant growth characteristics. Their stagnant or slow and negative population growth show that they are very poor in their functional stand. The stagnant or even the decline in pace of their population growth can be well judged in the sense that the small towns of 1901 fail to acquire even the total population growth rate for the region during the time span of 90 years.

The above description finds support from Fig. 10. in which the population growth of individual small towns has been shown in a graph.

Growth Pattern Perspectives : Temporal Phase Assessment :

A full comprehension of the growth behaviour of small towns in its spatio- temporal dimension, is, however, required in the analysis of phased decadal variation. The temporal variations in growth rates show connections with the arithmetical consequences of small population base or recent speed that the individual town tends to achieve in certain regional unit. The following are the observations that come out of these variations :

1. Over all pace behaviour in urbanisation prompts to deduce a tendency in which the growth of small towns moves slowly. stagnantly or negatively.
2. Distinct temporal phases of growth range variations in small towns are discernible.
3. Successive temporal phases reflect a tendency of acceleration of growth.
4. Dynamics of small towns growth expresses eventful behaviours and tendencies of steadiness and spatial decentralisation.
5. The growth behaviour tends to express the marked deviation with reference to the preceding decade of 1971-81. The newly formed administrative units, general trend of decentralisation of developmental measures and associated results and growing fascination of urban life have made such a deviation to set in.

While studying the trend of growth of small towns of North Bihar Plain, for distinct phases have been marked:

Negative Growth (1901-21)—By 1921 the region shows about 20 per cent decline in the population of small towns, over 1901. The causes of such negative growth may be correlated with the prevalence of endemic and epidemics, famines and droughts, etc. before 1921. Lalganj witnessed a fall in its population by- 21.11 percent and -21.23 per cent and Rosera by-19.74 and -0.44 per cent during 1901-11 and 1911-21 decades respectively whereas Mirganj was declassified in 1921.

Slow Growth (1921-41)—The period from 1921-41 has been that of slow urbanization, showing positive growth rates for the small towns of the region except the negative growth of Jainagar (-34.27 per cent) during the decade of 1931-41 which emerged as only one small town for the region in 1921. The average decadal growth rate of small towns in the region was below 10 per cent. The highest and lowest decadal growth rates during the said period were 22.06 per cent and 3.25 per cent for Lalganj during 1921-31 and 1931-41 respectively. This obviously means that the period between 1921 and 1941 has not been marked by an incentive which could gear up growth potentiality.

Medium Growth (1941-61) :—Post-independence period witnesses and increasing trend of urbanisation throughout the region as a result of growing economic base and agricultural development. The small towns have shown a steady increase during the period. The total number of small towns raised to 8 and 4 in 1951 and 1961 respectively. During 1941-51 all the 4 small towns have shown positive growth rates. The highest decadal growth rate was 61.65 per cent for Jainagar and the lowest was 13.08 per cent for Chanpatia. During 1951-61, except the negative growth of -31.39 per cent for regained urban status of small town Mirganj, all the small towns have shown positive growth rates ranging between a high of 118.49 per cent for Chanpatia and a low of 2.49 per cent for Chakia. It is noticeable that except Chanpatia and Dalsinghsarai (59.65%) remaining all small towns have shown an average growth rate below 15 per cent but this has surpassed 1941 figures by a comfortable margin.

Rapid Growth (1961 onwards) :—The period between 1961-91 records maximum increase in the formation of new towns. In 1971 three and in 1981 eight new towns were added to the total number of small towns. Birpur in Saharsa district came to be classed in 1961 as one such small town which stands as a planned townscape. It was developed particularly due to the massive work of Kosi project. During 1961-71, the small towns of the region witnessed an average growth rate below 15 per cent due to the negative growth rates of few towns e.g. Chakia (-50.18 per cent), Chanpatia (-16.28 per cent), dalsingsarai (-14.28 per cent) and Jogbani (-0.32 per cent), etc. The highest population increase during this period was in Banmankhi Bazar, which was 32.91 per cent. The population increase of small towns during 1971-81 had a remarkable pace. All the towns have shown positive growth rates ranging between a high of 223.47 per cent for Chakia and a low of 14.67 percent for Dalsingsarai. During the last decade of 1971-81, except the newly emerged 8 small towns which have not been taken for consideration in growth characteristics description, 5 among the remaining 16 recorded more than 50 percent decadal population growth. These towns are Chakia, Jogbani (109.16%), Banmankhi Bazar (88.63%), Mairwa (76.46 %) and Sugauli (61.59%).

The decade 1981-91 stands in marked contrast to the preceding decade of 1971-81. The population of small towns in the region which were 3,66,143 in 1981 rose to 3, 79, 829 in 1991- a gain of only 3.74 per cent during the last decade. A nominal over all increase in its population may be attributed to an appreciable decennial increase in the size of population of 11 small towns of 1981 which have been recorded as class III towns in 1991. Further, the most spectacular has been increase in the formation of small towns as in 1991. 13 new towns were added to the list. This has been due mainly to expansion of economic activities and transportation link with various trade centres in and around their respective district headquarters giving fillip to its urban structure. This clearly indicates visible signs in its infrastructure that may increase absolute population of the existing small towns as well as rise in its number in the coming decades.

Progressive, Stagnant and Decaying Towns :— The small towns under study have been classified into three categories e.g. Progressive, stagnant and decadent based on their growth between 1901-91 period. The 13 new towns added in 1991 are not taken into consideration in this classification. Out of the remaining 14, 6 small towns have been termed as progressive and 8 as stagnant. No small town is now decandent. Progressive towns are those which exhibited an annual growth rate of more than 3 percent in their population (about the average per annum growth rate of population of the North Bihar Plain during 1901-91).

The decadent towns record a decrease (negative growth), while the towns of stagnant type mark negligible growth of below 2 per cent per annum in their population.

Mairwa (2.94%), Dalsinghsarai (2.74%), Birpur (2.76%), Thakurganj (2.63%), Jainagar (2.54%), Mohiuddinnagar (2.51%), Maharajganj (2.16%) and Mirganj (1.15%) annual growth rate are classed as stagnant towns.

It is notable that except few small towns e.g. Nirmali (5.14 % annual growth rate), Belsand 3%), Chanpatia (6.31%) and Manihari (3.70% annual growth rate) remaining all small towns of the progressive group have shown only a marginal population increase in comparison with those of the stagnant group. Most of the progressive small towns emerged as urban centres particularly after independence. Janakpur Road (Pupri) the only town recording a negative growth of -37.18 per cent during 1971-81 (-3.72% per annum) has been recognised as a progressive town of the region in 1991. The short urban history of their growth is one of the most important points for having more percentile annual increase. Details of the individual town-growth characteristics are evident from the Fig. 5 and tables 3.2 (A) & (B).

Variation in the growth rates of towns is more or less a universally accepted phenomenon. The observation that practically the "slow growth is attributed to a low administrative status, poor transport connectivity, inadequate developmental efforts and fast growth of some large towns in close proximity"[5] find support incase of small towns of North Bihar Plain as well.

It has been observed in Indian urbanisation in general and same for the area under study that the population of the urban centres is increasing more or less proportionate to their class[6]. Like the general national and state level trends in the region under study also the rate of population growth of large urban centres is faster than the total urbanisation. On the other side, the small towns exhibit the most sluggish growth. The slower pace of their urbanisation is probably a result of their declassification decay and stagnant growth. Many such small towns have vast potential for the planned developments at the regional and sub-regional levels.

Therefore, the survey and analysis of small towns in the regional frame-work is a call of time.

Table 3.2 (A)

Size Rank of small towns 1981	Growth Period	Total Growth in percent	Annual Growth rate in percent
1.	1951-81	114.81	3.83
2.	1901-81	62.72	0.87
3.	1961-81	22.26	2.23
4.	1971-81	16.30	1.63
5.	1901-81	303.07	3.79
6.	1961-81	108.55	5.43
7.	1961-81	150.72	7.82
8.	1901-81	73.30	0.72
10.	1961-81	70.63	3.82
12.	1941-81	256.10	6.40
14.	1961-81	40.70	2.35
15.	1951-81	70.30	2.36
16.	1961-81	60.70	3.35
18.	1921-81	95.56	1.59
19.	1961-81	76.56	7.66
22	1961-81	98.00	4.90
23	1951-81	58.17	1.94
25.	1961-81	-37.18	-3.72

No. refers to size rank of small towns as in Appendix (II) The missing numbers refer to newly emerged towns in 1981 in the case of table 3.2 (A) and 1991 in the case of table 3.2 (B)

The small towns of North Bihar Plain may serve as counter magnet to the existing large urban cities of Purnea, Katihar, Muzaffarpur, Darbhanga and Chapra and large towns like Saharsa, Bettiah, Motihari etc. Even if a fraction of migrants to these large urban centres could be diverted towards these small towns, with the enhancement of local as well some exotic resources their in, they will help in integrating area planning and development as well as more orderly urbanisation is the state in general and in the North Bihar Plain in particular. This, indeed, is the idea of decentralization.

Renovation and reactivisation of the existing small towns with the development of additional generative forces, is although a costly affair, but a must for balanced economic/urban growth since they not only affect the industrial and agro-industrial sphere but also the agricultural and rural development by providing improved service facilities.

Table 3.2 (B)

Sl. No.	Name of Small towns	Size Rank 1991	Size of population (year)	Size population 1991	Total growth rate%	Annual growth rate %
1.	Mirganj	1	9698(1901)	19697	103.10	1.15
2.	Chanpatia	2	8544(1971)	19320	126.12	6.31
3.	Manihari	5	12592(1981)	17252	37.0	3.70
4.	Maharajganj	6	9214(1951)	17165	86.29	2.16
5.	Dalsingh-Sarai	9	7953(1951)	16738	110.46	2.76
6.	Mairwa	11	8033(1961)	15215	89.41	2.94
7.	Birpur	12	8061(1961)	14742	82.88	2.76
8.	Belsand	13	10804(1981)	14151	30.97	3.10
9.	Nirmali	15	5423(1961)	13783	154.16	5.14
10.	Chakia	16	6551(1961)	13708	109.25	3.64
11.	Thakurganj	17	10760(1981)	13589	26.29	2.63
12.	Mohiuddinnagar	23	8805(1981)	11012	25.06	2.51
13	Janakpur Road	25	6943(1981)	9590	38.12	3.81
	North Bihar Plain		31445 (1901)	379826	-	-

Source : Complied and calculated from Census of India (1991): Series-4 : Bihar: Towns Directory, Part XA and Town-wise Primary Census Abstract, 1991

The above analysis of growth characteristics of small towns of North Bihar Plain leads to several broad findings which include:—

(i) In general, the growth of small towns in the region is stagnant. That can be correlated with the lower level of urbanisation, i.e. only about a half of state (Bihar) and quarter of national level of urbanisation.

(ii) The small towns of recent origin have shown comparatively faster growth than the old ones as the recent pace of urbanisation has also got momentum in district of North Bihar Plain, e.g. out of 19 districts of the region except 4 (Paschimi Champaran-23.37%, Vaishali-38.64%, Begusarai- 45.22%, Darbhanga-33.18%) all the districts have shown the average or more than the state average growth of urban population during 1971-81.

(iii) The regional distribution of small towns and their growth-both show concentration in a few district which recorded high level of urbanization in recent decades. The regional pattern of slow growth of small towns appears to be correlated with the regional pattern of urbanization.

(iv) Most of the stagnant or slow growing small towns are localised in fast or moderate urban growth districts indicating that some of the fast growing urban centres growing at the cost of others.

(v) Most of the slow growing small towns have long urban features.

(vi) Except the preceding decade of 1981-91, all the small towns have shown either fluctuating decadal growth rate or have experienced negative growth rate in any previous decade.

(vii) There are several reason for out migration and hence for slow a growth of small towns. In general while slow population growth of towns appears to be associated with the low level of administrative status, poor transport connectivity and inadequate planned developmental efforts are the other factors. There is no clear cut relationship between the economy of these towns and their slow growth.

(viii) One of the major causes of slow urban growth of a small town is related to a faster growth of a nearby town implying that slow growth is not only a result of the growth potential of the town itself but is also determined by the shape of development processes working in the micro-regional economy.

The above analysis of growth behaviour of small towns of the region reveal the fluctuating fortunes of their growth history. An overall trend reveals that in general the small towns of the region have established their continuity of growth right from the time of independence. This observation finds support with the result obtained from the calculation of growth indices of small towns in the region as mentioned in the following caption.

Growth Indices of Small Towns:—

The growth indices of small towns in the region has been worked out by using the formula

$$GI = \frac{P_2 x100}{P_1}$$

Where P_2 = Population of small towns in the region in recent decade.
(i.e. Year for which the G1 is required)

P_1 = Base year C i.e. 1901 in present context)

Details of the growth indices are evidence at from the table- 3.3. The above table shows that the, growth indices of small towns in the region during various decades include two district phases, viz. (i) Pre-independence period and (ii) Post-independence period. The growth indices of pre-independence period during various decades show the trend of relegating growth while the figures of post independence period point to promising growth indices. However considering the agriculture-oriented economy of the region and increasing number of small towns since independence, the recent decades figures are encouraging.

Table 3.3

North Bihar Plain: Growth Indices of Small Towns

years	No. of Small Towns in the region	Total Population of small towns	Growth Indices
1901	3	31445	100.00
1911	3	25386	80.73
1921	3	21448	68.21
1931	3	24639	78.36
1941	4	28482	90.58
1951	8	7303.8	232.27
1961	14	137863	526.48
1971	17	196997	554.71
1981	25	366143	1064.18
1991	27	379826	1107.91

Source : Complied from census of India (1981): Series- 4 : Bihar, Town Directory, Part-XA and Towns wise primary Census Abstract, 1991.

Estimation of Growth of Small Towns :— "In view of the cause-quential problems that are created by the process of urbanisation, there has been a growing concern amongst the policy makers, administrators, planners and others about the trend, direction and dimensions of urban growth "[7].

The significant role of small towns "serving as an intermediary between the village and metropolis"[8] is bound to play an active part in the human habitat system. The rate of growth of small towns may be treated as the indicator of regional growth pattern.

Observations and generalisations are supported more by qualitative and optimistic deductions rather than quantitatively projected and correlated evidences. Reasons are obviously connected with technical difficulties associated with projections and technicality of statistical analysis. Population increment lacks any fixed 'law', various projection methods yield widely varying results. Unreliability of information on 'population process mortality, fertility and migration"[9] and total inadequacy of economic and social indices put limitations on such projection techniques which rely on correlation of population numbers with social and economic indices and set the projection "frought and uncertainties"[10]. Still their value is to be viewed in planning purposes by making them approximate to the rationality.

Table 3.4

Small Towns : Future Population Estimates

Sl.	Name of Town	Actual	Estimated Population in (,000)			
			2001		2011	
		Population 1991 (in,000)	Arithmetic progression	Geometric progression	Aritmetic progression	Geometric progression
1.	Mirganj	19.7	21.2	21.5	22.7	23.5
2.	Chanpatia	19.3	24.7	29.0	30.1	43.6
3.	Katihar Rly. Col.	18.9	23.6	23.6	29.3	29.3
4.	Motipur	17.8	22.2	22.2	27.6	27.6
5.	Manihari	17.3	21.9	23.7	26.6	32.4
6.	Maharajganj	17.2	19.3	19.8	21.4	23.1
7.	Jainagar	17.0	18.7	19.9	20.4	23.2
8.	Chchatapur	16.7	20.8	20.8	26.0	26.0
9.	Dalsingsarai	16.7	18.9	20.2	21.2	24.2
10.	Kanti	16.0	20.0	20.0	24.8	24.8
11.	Mairwa	15.2	19.1	22.8	23.6	34.1
12.	Birpur	14.7	17.0	18.0	19.2	22.0
13.	Belsand	14.2	17.5	18.4	20.8	24.0
14.	Sheohar	13.9	17.3	17.3	21.6	21.6
15.	Nirmali	13.8	16.6	18.9	19.3	25.7
16.	Chakia	13.7	16.1	17.6	18.5	22.4
17.	Thakurganj	13.6	16.4	17.0	19.2	21.5
18.	Kataiya	13.3	16.6	16.6	20.6	20.6
19.	Barauni I.O.C.	12.6	15.8	15.8	19.6	19.6
20.	Ghoghardiha	12.0	15.0	15.0	18.6	18.6
21.	Dumra	11.6	14.5	14.5	18.0	18.0
22.	Samastipur Rly. Col.	11.6	14.4	14.4	18.0	18.0
23.	Mohiuddinnagar	11.0	13.2	13.8	15.4	17.2
24.	Rajoptti Talkhapur	10.8	13.4	13.4	16.7	16.7
25.	Janakpur Road	9.6	12.2	12.2	14.9	14.9
26	Lauthaha	5.8	7.2	7.2	9.0	9.0
27.	Bhimnagar	5.7	7.1	7.1	8.8	8.8
	North Bihar Plain	379.8	461.1	180.7	552.3	620.1

To obtain projected population for these towns simple projection techniques of N.g. method, Arithmetic Progression, Geometric, progression, Incremental increase method, etc. have been considered. different methods give quite different results.

The developmental potentiality and general nature of growth trend of the individiual town have been considered as main points for applying the different methods. The final result is the outcome of both the quantitative and qualitative analysis. Estimated population for 2001 and 2011 have thus been tabulated for small towns of North Bihar Plain in Table 3.4.

Small towns of North Bihar Plain will increase population with a modest per annum increase in many cases and appreciable per annum growth in some cases. In general, the small towns of North Bihar Plain with average decadal increase of 3.75 per cent during 1981-91 will contain 481 thousands and 620 thousands of population by 2001 and 2011 respectively.

The estimated growths of newly formed urban centres have been calculated on the basis of general and average growth trend of small towns of the region, which has been worked out 24.50 per cent per decade or 2.45 per cent per annum.

It goes without saying that during course of population increase existing small towns will change their size-class too. Table 3.1 shows that at least 11 out of 25 small towns of 1981 have moved to class III status in 1991. Similarly, 08 in out of 27 small towns of 1991 will join hands with them by 2001 (cf. Table 3.4).

The newly formed administrative headquarters e.g. C.D. Block and sub-division headquarters, market centres and nodes of transport services may contribute to the formation of new small towns. Small towns of North Bihar Plain as a result of development proposals have the potential to emerge as growth centres and as growth points to form part of hierarchy of Growth Foci in Bihar.

In recent years, numerous countries have attempted to implement growth-centre or growth area policies for the purposes of revitalizing depressed industrial areas dominated by stagnating or declining sectors and of stimulating economic development in region which have always lagged behind their countries more advanced regions. In many of these cases, governments have also been trying to divert migration-streams away from large, congested cities.

North Bihar Plain with appreciable number of existing small towns is a proper regions for this type of planned development because despite inperfections, "growth centre theory at least does offer the possibility of a fresh approach to problems of urban and regional development"[11]. "The government of India had also announced on June 3, 1988, its decision to set up 100 growth centre throughout the country over the next five years or 80"[12].

North Bihar Plain provides better places as small towns for a good number of such centres establishment because the following criteria shall be followed for selection of growth centres:-

(a) The growth centres shall be located close to District/Sub-Division/Block/Taluk Headquarters or developing urban centres, and

(b) The growth centres shall have access to the following basic facilities:-

i) Proximity to better transport facilities,

ii) Dependable water and power supply,

iii) Availability of responsible educational and health facilities,

iv) Growth centres should not be located in ecologically sensitive areas and they should not lead to denudation of the forests.

Small towns of North Bihar Plain have been comprehended with due reason to form the fundamental component of growth foci system. This is discussed in chapter V:

References

1. Garnier, J.B. & Chabot, G. 1967 '**Urban Geography**' Longman Green & Co. Ltd., London, p. 8

2. Mumford, L. 1961 '**The** City **in History**' London, p. 125.

3. Dickinson, R.E. 1971 'City and Region' Routledge & Kegan Paul Ltd. London, p. 19

4. Jha, S.N. 1989 'Small Towns of Bihar' A Study in Urban Regional Planning Strategy, Approved Ph. D. Thesis, L. N. Mithila University, p. 24.

5. Pathak, p 1986 '**Slow Growing Towns in India**', *Population Geography*' Vol. 8, No.1 & 2, June- Dec. 1986, p. 64

6. Dube, K.K. & Singh, M.B. 1979 Growth of Small Towns in Eastern

U.P. : A Geographical Study, Place of Small Towns in India (ed) R.L. Singh & Rana P. B. Singh, N.G.S.I. Varanasi, p. 166

7. Lal, B.B. 1986 : '**Town Directory, Census of India**' Part X-A, New Delhi, p.5

8. Manshard, W. 1979 '**Foreword**' on "**Place of Small Towns in India (ed.) R. L. Singh** Rana P. B. Singh, N.G.S.I. Varanasi, p.3

9. Heer, D.M. 1969 '**Society and Population**' Prentice Hall of India, Pvt. Ltd., New Delhi, pp. 34-79

10. Ram, L.N. 1969 Impact of population Growth of Lands of Bihar, '**Eassays in Geography**, (ed) K. N. Das, Bhagalpur University, Bhagalpur, p. 130

11. Hanson, Niles M. 1971 '**Intermediate-size Cities as Growth Centres**', Praeger Publishers, New York, p. 14

12. '**Employment News**' 1988 'Employment News' Dec. 10, 1988, New Delhi, p. 2

Chapter-IV

Socio-Economic Characteristics

The present study comprises social and economic characteristics of the 27 small towns of North Bihar Plain. It includes the analysis of age, sex, literacy and education and other demographic features which are greatly influenced by economic behaviour of a settlement, e.g. worker ratio, occupational structure, skill and enterpreneurship etc.

There is no denying the fact that 'town' is the vortex of economic uplift and social change in a community'[1]. This brings forth the importance of urban development as an integral part of socio-economic planning. It is, therefore, essential to study the impact of these factors so as to accelerate the tempo of urban development which in turn would call for an uphill task of town planning in an organised way for the stagnent small-urban-centres in the region under study.

Age-Structure : Age structure is a biological population characteristics. There are three basic determinants of age composition of a population, viz. fertility, mortality and mobility. Clarke rightly points out that these three determinants of age structure are inter dependent and any change in one of those may influence the other two and it is through these variables that the socio-economic conditions influence the age structure.[2]

Despite immense significance of age structure, its study, particularly of small towns, has suffered a neglect. Detailed 1991 census data related to age composition of small towns are not available. It seems, therefore, imperative to examine all the relevant aspects of the district level data of age-groups of total urban population as they do reveal some highly significant trends and differentials as the sequel will show. Age pyramids (1981) showing the age and sex composition of urban population of Bihar are revealing many things. The table 4.1 shows the percentage of total juvenile, young, middle and old & elderly persons for both the sexes.

Table 4.1
Age Structure of Urban Population, 1981
(Figures represent percentage of total urban Population)

Types	Age-Groups	Bihar		North Bihar Plain	
		Male	Female	Male	Female
Juvenile (infants, boys & girls)	0-14	20.79	18.96	21.34	18.92
II. Young	15-34	18.86	15.16	17.82	14.38
III. Middle-Aged	35-59	12.33	8.14	11.48	10.81
IV. Old & Elderly Persons	60& above	2.64	3.12	3.22	2.67

Source : Census of India, 1981 : Series - : Bihar, Part-IV **Social and Cultural Tables.**

An analysis of data given above shows that percentage of juvenile population is 21.34 and 18.92 in 1981 for the male and female sexes respectively. This taken together is higher by 0.51 percent than Bihar. The ratios of young men and women in the age-group 15-34 are only 17.82 and 14.83 in the region under study, which is lower than the state average by 1.82 per cent. Middle aged persons (35-59), on the other hand, constituted 11.48 and 10.18 per cent for the two sexes respectively. Again, proportion of old & elderly persons in the region exceeds the average for the state, particularly in the case of females. These statistics amply indicate ill-balanced age-structure of its population. This issue has been clearly pointed out by Prof.. Dayal in the Indian context [3].

Further, as is evident from available 1991 age data (population of children below 6 years) of small towns, high fertility usually leads to a population structure heavily weighted in the juvenile age group in the region. The proportion of children (below 6 years) is markedly high in both sexes: males (18.0) and females (19.58) and significantly this large population represents for the most part, an economically un-productive segment, which must be fed, clothed, housed an educated. Hence, this represents a serious economic burden for the poor in the already stagnating urban economy of small towns in the region.

Further, proportion of children (under 6 years) shows fairly notable regional variations among 27 small towns in the region. Nevertheless, it is the most dominant group in the age structure of the population of the individual small town as well as that of the region as a whole. By keeping the regional average of 18.73 per cent in view, the whole region may be divided broadly into three distinct regions in 1991. The high percentage zone (above 20) includes as many as 10 small towns namely Mirganj, Motipur, Manihari, Chchatapur, Kanti, Belsand, Sheohar, Chakia, Kataiya and Rajopatti Talkhapur. Children of fair sex out number male sex in all of them. Some 8 small towns, viz. Katihar Railway Colony, Birpur, Barauni Indian Oil corporation, Dumra, Samastipur Railway Colony, Janakpur Road, Lauthaha and Bhimnagar have relatively low percentage (below 18) of children, below the regional average. Remaining 9 small towns fall under the moderate category of 18-20 percent. There is not much difference in its distributional pattern of both sexes.

These variations are not to be taken accidental. They follow a certain descertible pattern and reflect, in some measure, the impact and diversity of socio-economic conditions. Small towns with different degrees of socio-economic development have definite impact on their pattern. Disparity also occurs between areas of backward agrarian economy and diversified agricultural economic base of these small towns. In order to appreciate fully the above two fold significance of the age-structure the economic composition of these small towns will place things in right perspective in the pages that follow.

Sex Ratio:—Sex is another important biological population characteristics. The most commonly used technique for expressing the sex ratio is as follows :—

$$\text{Sex ratio (Sr.)} = \frac{\text{Number of Females}}{\text{Numbers of males}} \times 100$$

Urban centres in general present the 'young' and 'male' characteristics of population. In most of the Indian cities there is male population predominance over the females population. But in the Latin American cities there is a clear cut preponderance of females over males. It is owing to the social and economic factors that contribute to a great extent the sex-ratios in these cities.[4]

In North Bihar Plain sex ratio has been worked out at 920:1000 and 856:1000 for rural and urban area respectively as against 915:1000 for an average total population according 1991 census. Small towns of the region under study falling quite in line with the general features have higher proportion of male population. The differentials in sex ratio of small towns show an over all negative relation with their size class hierarchy, i.e. the higher the class the lower the sex ratio and vice-versa. In general, the feature of lower sex ratio in urban areas in comparison to that in the rural area is due to the fact that town attracts the male population by way of employment opportunities. The female population continues to stay in the villages. Higher cost of living in urban areas is another factor that discourages people from shifting the entire family to the urban areas. Class V and VI towns of the region have contrastingly low sex ratio than those of other categories of towns. These towns exhibit a significant deficiency of females in their population. The evidence and type of migration a particular town is experiencing may be attributed to explain to a large extent the pattern of sex composition of its towns in the region.

Table 4.2 shows that the ratio of females was high in class IV followed by class III towns during all these four decades. These towns were generally medium in size and agricultural and commercial in nature. The ratio was very low in class VI towns because they were small industrial and administrative towns. In these towns the working population generally consisted of males. They were engaged in industries, construction and professional jobs. Most of them had mainly immigrated and left their families behind in their villages. The low sex ratio in class I towns may be attributed to high male percentage among the service holders as well as a shortage of houses in them.

Table 4.2

Sex Ratio of all classes of towns in North Bihar Plain 1961-91

Year	North Bihar Plain	Classes of Towns I	II	III	IV	V	VI
1961	818	776	787	835	860	803	501
1971	822	802	805	813	873	827	603
1981	848	836	834	861	879	792	-
1991	856	842	848	866	868	730	-

Source : Compiled and computed from Census of India : Series 4: Bihar Town Directory.

In the census of 1961, the highest ratio of females was found in class IV followed by class III towns, i.e. 860:1000 and 835:1000 respectively. These figures were more than the average for the region 818:1000. All the other four categories of towns had a low ratio of females.

In the census of 1971, the female ratio was higher in Class IV and V categories, i.e. 873:1000 and 827: 1000 respectively followed by class III towns with 813:1000. The lowest ratio was again found in class VI towns, viz. 603:1000 and were most masculine in character. There were two towns in class I category and both had almost equal ratio of females which were lower than the average of the region, i.e. 822:1000. Mahnar Bazar (Now class III) was the only town which had more than one thousand females, i.e. 1007 : 1000. The towns of class IV like Revelganj, Kasba, Lalganj had more than the average ratio of the region, i.e. 973, 930 and 924 respectively followed by Nirmali with 930 (class V towns). All these are primary towns and their details are given at a later stage. Again the lowest ratio was found in Lauthaha, Dumra and Birpur, i.e. 404, 647 and 722 respectively.

In the 1981 Census, the highest ratio of females is found again in class IV and III towns followed by Class I and Class II towns. There are no class VI towns in 1981 in the region. All the class VI towns grown in to the class V towns as the sizes of these towns swelled up with ever increasing population. So the lowest ratio of females is found in Class V towns. The highest female ratio is found in newly born towns of 1981, i.e. Mohiuddinnagar (1006) and Barauli (986) followed by older towns like Revelganj, Mahnar Bazar, Teghra (976, 972 and 969 females respectively). It shows that where agriculture has remained predominant among occupations the ratio of females is generally high.

The salient features of the sex ratio of small towns in the region as per 1991 census revealed broadly the 1981 pattern. Although on an average the small towns of the study region have a sex ratio of 860, yet it varies from the lowest of 658 in Lauthaha to the highest of 936 in Maharajganj. Old small towns of the region such as Maharajganj (936), Mohiuddinnagar (930), Dalsingsarai (908) and Mirganj (900) display high sex ratio and the explanations are not far to seek as the out migration of males to neighbouring towns of Chapra, Samastipur and Patna, particularly after the construction of the "Gandhi Setu" over the river Ganga is largely responsible for giving this feminine character to them. On the other extreme, some new towns in 1991 such as Lauthaha (658), Bhimnagar (663), Katihar Railway Colony (797), have relative deficiency of females. They are emerging trade and commercial-cum administrative towns where their female counterparts prefer to reside at their nearby villages. A wide range of variations in sex ratio is found among the small towns of North Bihar Plain as is evident from table 4.3 (A & B).

Table 4.3 (A).

Sex Ratio of small towns, 1981

Sex Ratio Range	Nature & Degree	Small Towns (sex Ratio)	Total No.s of Towns
Below 800	Low	16 (726,), 25 (779)	2
800-899	Moderate	7 (801), 21 (809) 6 (821), 18 (839) 10 (842), 23 (854) 1 (861) 22 (865) 4 (881), 17 (884) 8 (886), 20 (891) and 12 (893)	13
900-999	High	11 (901), 19 (907) 5 (913), 9 (916) 3 (917), 2 (934) 14 (938), 13 (944) 15 (944)	9
1000 & Above		24 (1006)	1
			25

Nos refer to size Rank of Small Towns as in 1981. Appendix-II

Sex Ratio may be treated as an indicator of the functional specialization of towns. Barring a few exceptions, towns having low sex ratio represent the dominance of non-agricultural development base at one hand and town having high sex ratio bear the testimony of the dominance of agricultural base on the other, this ultimately reveals their developmental potentialities. After seeing these ratios of females and males during the last four decades and separately calculated through 1991 census, we come to the conclusion that the males ratio is increasing steadily as table 4.2 reveals. In Class V towns where the ratio was already very low, it is further decreasing. However, in the towns which have better educational, medical and residential facilities, the females tend to immigrate and as a result the ratio becomes more balanced.[5] This is also due to high female literacy in the larger towns. Services and professional jobs are also easily available for females who may even live Singly without families in such towns. So the recent trend is that the female ratio is going up.

Table 4.3 (B)
North Bihar Plain : Sex Ratio of Small Towns, 1991

Sex Ratio Range	Pattern	Name of Small Towns with Sex Ratio in brackets	Frequency
Below 800	Low	3 (798), 12 (972) 21 (778), 22 (773) 26 (658), 27 (663)	06
800-900	Moderate	2 (888), 4 (881), 5 (892), 7, (873) 8 (888), 10 (875) 11 (877), 13 (858) 14 (860), 15 (873) 16 (842), 17 (868) 18 (879), 19 (874) 24 (856), 25 (823)	16
Above 900	High	1 (900), 6 (936) 9 (908), 20 (912) 23 (930)	05
			27

Source : Census of India, Bihar, Town wise P.C.A. 1991, N.I.C. Unit Patna.

*No refers to size rank of small towns as in 1991.

LITERACY & EDUCATION:—Literacy is that cultural attribute of population which is fairly a reliable index of the socio-economic development of an area. Universal literacy and higher education which are generally correlated with such traits of modern civilization as urbanization, industrialization, communications and commerce are indispensable to the advancement of nations in the present day world.[6] Educational attainment thus ranks high in importance among the various qualities of a population. The towns of North Bihar Plain have not so far attained complete literacy, though they are in an active process of reaching the stage or addressing the problems very earnestly. However, literacy does not necessarily increase with the size of towns in the study region. Perhaps the

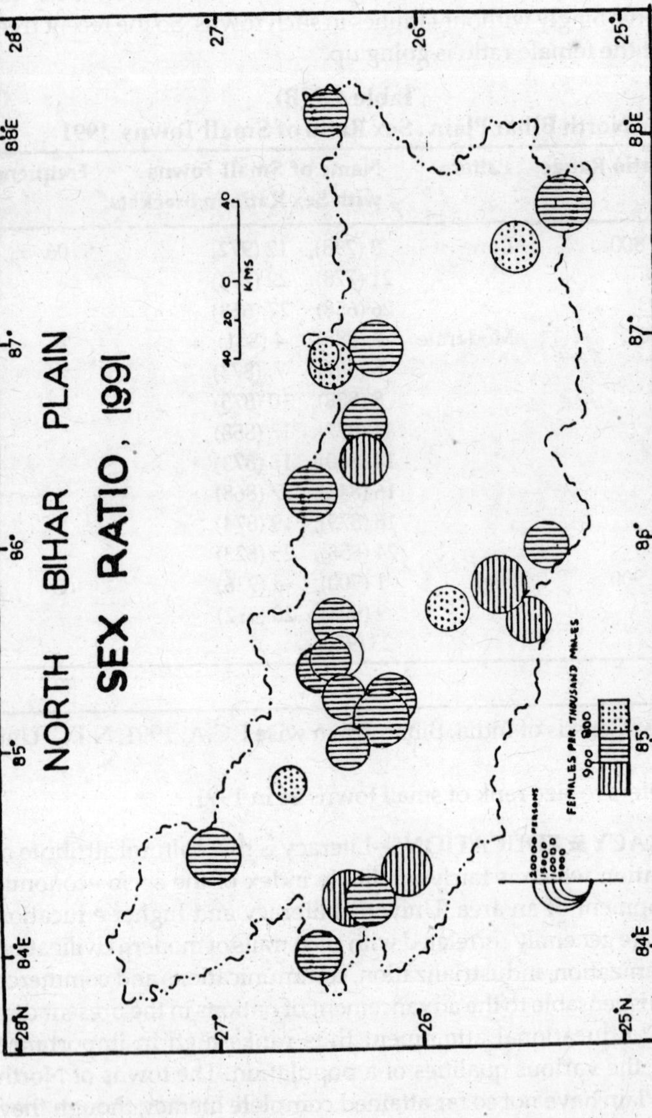
NORTH BIHAR PLAIN
SEX RATIO, 1991
40 20 0 40
KMS
FEMALES PER THOUSAND MALES
900 900
20000 PERSONS
15000
10000
5000
28N
27
26
25N
28
27
26
25
84E
85
86
87
88E

Fig. 11

largest cities have the heaviest rural-urban migration and therefore, draw a larger proportion of their citizens from the relatively illiterate countryside.[7] This holds equally good in the present case.

Bihar is one of the least literate states of India, and has only 38.48 per cent of the total population in 1991 literate as against the 52.21 Percent of national average. The area of North Bihar Plain, further, shows its more backwardness than the state average in this trait. Hardly a little over one-third (38.5%) of the population in the region in literate. Among the districts of North Bihar Plain the percentage of effective literacy as in 1991 ranges from a high of 41.8 for Saran district to a low of 22.2 per cent for Kishanganj district.[8]

Table 4.4

Literacy of All Classes of Towns in North Bihar Plain : 1961-1991

Years	North Bihar Plain	Classes of Towns I	II	III	IV	V	VI
1961	38.41	46.13	42.46	37.66	32.36	32.88	57.75
1971	39.74	46.93	42.19	39.27	32.46	37.96	55.69
1981	46.37	53.93	48.57	43.19	37.38	51.26	-
1991	49.97	58.23	56.64	44.67	44.75	52.18	-

Source : Compiled and computed from different Censuses.

Table 4.4 shows that literacy is increasing in the towns of the region day by day. The region had 38.41 per cent literacy in 1961, 39.74 per cent in 1971, 46.37 per cent in 1981 and 49.97 per cent in 1991. There was an increase of 1.33 per cent during 1961-71, which rose to 6.63 per cent in the period 1971-81 and further to 3.6 percent in the preceding decade. This shows that literacy is increasing at a faster pace. The female literacy, however, increased only from 12.01 per cent in 1971 to 15.38 per cent in 1981 and 22.89 per cent in 1991. So the rise in female literacy is slower than that for the males.

Among the different classes of towns in the region, the literacy is seen to be higher in class II and I towns in 1991.

Generally, the lowest literacy was recorded in Class IV towns. A fact that urban literacy is always higher than the rural and naturally, therefore, towns have higher percentage of literate and educated persons than the countryside in a district. Small towns of North Bihar Plain have well above 45 percent of their population which may be considered as literate as against the 58 percent and 51 per cent for class I and medium size towns of the region under study respectively. It is noticeable that until recently, literacy in India meant male literacy to a great extent and the region under study is not exception to this general understanding. The gap between male and female literacy is about 18 per cent in the region. This unusual disparity is the result of a long continued prejudice against the education of women and also against their employment out side the home.[9] However, these prejudices have been disappearing rather rapidly in recent years, though much remains to be desired.

The variation of literacy among small towns of North Bihar Plain is evident from table 4.5 and Fig 12. Literacy is very poor in the towns where agriculture is the predominating activity and it is high to very high in the manufacturing towns such as Barauni I.O.C. township. This higher literacy is also seen in administrative town-cum transport towns, e.g. Katihar and Samastipur railway Colonies which have a high percentage of literacy of over 71. The female literacy is also higher in these towns.

Table 4.5
North Bihar Plain
Pattern of Literacy of Small Towns, 1991*

Literacy Range %	Nature & Degree	Small towns (Size Rank)	Total Nos. of towns.
Below 30	Very Low	8, 13, 14	03
30.0 to 39.99	Low	2, 4, 5, 10 15, 18, 20 23, 24	09
40.0-49.99	Moderate	1, 6, 9, 11 16, 17, 25	07
50.0 & above	High	3, 7, 12, 19, 21, 22, 26, 27	08

* Nos. refer to size rank of small towns as in 1991.

Yet sex and age-composition and the size of families have even more striking effects upon educational and many other features of the cultural landscape. Further, proportion of SC population and literacy rate of small towns in the region bear no strong positive correspondence as is evident from the table given below :—

Table 4.6
Proportion of S.C. Population and Literacy Rates in some selected Small towns North Bihar Plain, 1991

Sl. No.	Name of Town	Proportion of SC Population	Literacy rate%
1.	Katihar Rly. Colony	17.25	71.78
2.	Jainagar	18.76	52.79
3.	Dalsingsarai	21.50	49.62
4.	Belsand	12.60	26.98
5.	Kanti	27.39	37.61
6.	Chchatapur	12.54	19.17
7.	Rajopatti Talkhapur	5.21	34.67

Source : Calculated by the author from Census of India, Bihar: Town wise P.C.A. data 1991, NIC Unit, Patna.

Male Literacy, 1991:—Effective male literacy rate of small towns in the region was 55.32 per cent and it varies from a maximum of 82.46 percent in Samastipur Railway Colony to a minimum of 27.59 per cent in Chachatapur town in the district of Saharsa. Detailed can be discerned from Fig. 12. Firstly, the rate of male literacy is high (over 60%) in 8 small towns due to urban impact, availability of educational facilities together with growing awareness among the dwellers. Secondly, male literacy rate is moderate (40 to 60%) in some 15 towns while it is low (below 40%) in 4 new small towns in the region. This may be attributed largely to low level of urbanization as well as lack of proper infrastructure for the spread of literacy. The rates fall much below the regional average.

Female Literacy, 1991:—Compared to their male counterpart female literates are still small in numbers as only a little over 37 percent of its females is literate. Secondly, there are wide areal variations as it varies between 66.89 per cent in Samastipur Railway Colony and 9.6 per cent in Chatapur towns in the region. Thirdly, out of 27 small towns the pattern of urban female literacy reads as under : (i) towns with high female literacy (above 40%) -07 towns, (ii) the moderate category (30 to 40%)-06 towns, (iii) low rate category (20 to 30%) -10 towns and (iv) towns with very low rate (below 20%)-04 towns.

Population of the old class IV towns are socially more awakened and economically more capable of imparting education to their female children than their newer and smaller counterparts The educational facilities available for girl students in the former, are

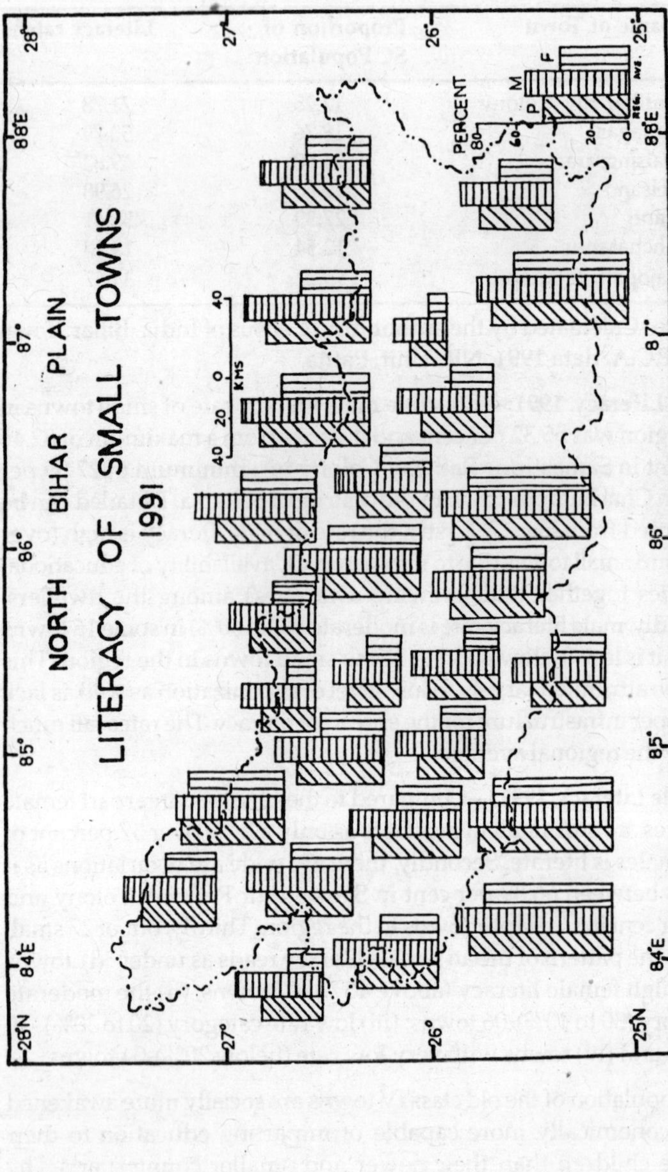
NORTH BIHAR PLAIN
LITERACY OF SMALL TOWNS
1991
PERCENT
P M F
KMS
28°N
27°
26°
25°N
84°E
85°
86°
87°
88°E
28°
25°

Fig. 12

decidely superior and efficient than those obtaining in the case of latter category of small towns. This will become clear from the sequel. Hence, sending girls to educational institution is also perceptible in the former category of towns in the area.

Male-Female differential in Literacy, 1991 :—We have observed just earlier the spatial pattern of male and female literacy in the region. An attempt has now been made to study indices of male-female differential in literacy in order that they give a meaningful picture in regional perspective. This differential study is based on index of differential (ID)[10]. which has been calculated as under:

$$ID = \frac{UMLR - UFLR}{TULR} \text{ of small towns}$$

Where ID = Index of differential

UMLR = Urban male Literacy rate.

UFLR = Urban Female Literacy rate.

TULR = Total Urban Literacy rate.

The indices of differential in its regional dimension have been analysed with the help of table given below:—

Table 4.7

Small Towns: Indices of Male-Female Differential in Literacy 1991.

D.I. Range	Pattern	Size Rank of Small towns	Nos.
0.10-0.30	Low	3, 19, 21, 22, 26	05
0.31-0.50	Moderate	7, 9, 12, 25	04
0.51-0.70	High	1, 2, 4, 5, 6, 10,	00
		11, 13, 16, 17, 20, 23	14
0.71 & above	Very High	8, 14, 15, 18	04
			27

One remarkable thing that is clear from the study is that as a matter of rule, the differntial indices have inverse relationship with urban literacy rates. This means that were literacy rate is high male-female differential index (DI) is low and where literacy is low DI is high. Poverty and backwardness may be singled out as the factors of great significance to explain the above pattern. Secondly, among 27 small towns of the region differential indices do vary greatly which clearly exemplify socio-economic level of their people. In the case of towns with agronomic and trade and commerce base together with lack of eagerness among females DI is high due abysmally low female literacy rate in them. Finally, this index is low in 05 small towns due to employment of females in areas of cultural and industrial development activities leading to better environment for their literacy.

Skill and Enterpreneurship :— Skill and enterpreneurship constitute the other two related components of study which are of greater significance in the development of the regional economy. Directorate of Technical Education, Government of Bihar plays a vital role in the establishment of skill formative institutions like Industrial Training Institute, Polytechnics, Cluster type training centres and many other vocational institutions. Small towns of Bihar, have very few such institutions and they need be expanded further.

Small towns have got to perform a number of important roles in the overall development of our country as a whole with special reference to economic growth. In the economy of agriculture-cum-industry frame work to be built in the country, small & medium towns will have to assume much added significance.

The policy of agricultural improvement and higher production will continue to be the basic strategy of a national economic growth and development. This will call not only the development of basic infrastructure like irrigation and transport network and powerlines all over the country. But also development of the chains of service of service centres to provide in put supply for production in the rural areas and to offer marketing facilities for produces. The location of supply centres for various inputs like seed and fertilizers, repair and servicing of agricultural implements, credit and banking facilities need to be such that these become accessible to the rural agricultural communities. These aspects of study are examined inthe chapter that follows.

The provision of various social, educational and health services, which are currently located at far off places, needs to be located at such centres that can be accessible to the users within reasonable travel distance. The development of various levels of educational. health and medical facilities may help in building the right type of skill and expertise in the rural population. The strategy of economic diversification is being advocated in the rural economy now heavily depended on agriculture. "The introduction of new cottage and small scale industries based on agriculture, forest or animal based products and the revival of traditional crafts, are expected to give highly satisfactory results in the economic growth"[11]. Development of input supply services to these rural based industries, marketing facilities for products and the skill-building training facilities etc. will be required to ensure these development processes.

Three points are noteworthy, firstly, small towns with primarily agricultural economy with low degree of commercialization and diversification have low literacy rates.

Secondly, there is lack of an in-built infrastructure in most of the small towns in the region and finally, the cultural contour of the people in the region needs to be changed in years to come through change in the attitude and behaviour of people inhabiting this backward agricultural region. All these will surely act s panacea to alleviase most of our social economic maladies.

Work Participation Rate:—The population may be dichotomised into two groups of: (i) economically active and (ii) economically inactive population.These two segments are of distinctive significance as thier proportion and economic composition have direct bearing on the pattern, rate and level of economic development in the region. It is in this context that the structure of the work force is intended to be examined with reference to participation rates by sexes and industrial categories.

Workers participation and their structural characterstics represent the salient features of a region's economy. History of settlement, right from " cave to village" to present modern urban edifices shows the bond of economic persuits. Not unnaturally, therefore, the two 'Urban Revolution'[12], the first ancient modest one, and the second modern speedy one establish link with the two revolutions-agricultural and industrial.[13] Towns are said to exist and prosper on account of their capacity to provide "opportunities for making a living, employment-greater in number and variety than in non-urban situations"[14]. Primary towns possess and agricultural out look and meet the primary needs of the people. This group includes the industrial workers categories I, II and III which affect farmland, the rural influence in the town and the labour force of variuós towns"[15]. This justification an attempt on the economic and functional behaviour of small towns for their developmental strategies. The most striking features in the manifold diversities of the economic and functional behaviour of the state's small towns lie in presence of their regional contrasts of economic base. A mosaic of various economics'[16] the plain Bihar and the Highland Bihar differ in having agricultural, forest and mineral resource bases respectively. The economy rears from rudimentary type of cultivation of the highly specialized manufacturing. The central weakness of the state's economy "lies is the poor agricultural base, which produce neither enough food for its rapidly growing population nor raw materials for its industry"[17]. Though nature has her compensation for both the geo-physical segments making agriculture, the basic of life in plain at its par excellence and the highland Bihar the natural home of forest and minerals. The economy of Bihar thus remains palpably dual, paradoxial and integrated in the lack of the achievements of healthy integration.

In the regional perspective, the small towns of North Bihar Plain reflect to very modest proportion of workers in their population. This is presented in the table 4.8.

Table 4.8
North Bihar Plain
Work Force of All Classes of Towns 1991

Classes of towns	Proportion of main Workers			Proportionof Marginal Workers		
	P	M	F	P	M	F
ClassI	23.36	39.85	3.78	0.13	0.06	0.21
ClassII	24.07	40.99	4.12	0.40	0.09	0.75
ClassIII	25.90	44.09	4.92	0.54	0.08	1.08
ClassIV	25.95	44.18	4.96	0.50	0.12	0.90
ClassV	25.50	41.44	3.68	0.005	0.001	0.01
ClassVI	-	-	-	-	-	-
Small Tows IV, V & VI	25.93	44.02	4.89	0.48	0.12	0.91

Source : Calculated by the author from census of India (1991), Bihar : **Town wise Primary Census Abstract,** NIC Unit, Patna.

The average perticipation rate of population of small towns was modest, relatively high than Class I and Class II towns in the region. The range of variation is less and runs from 20.64 per cent in Barauni I.O.C. township to 36.65 per cent in Chhatapur town. It is revealed that as many as 15 of its 27 small towns are areas of low proportion of workers and manage to accomodate themselves in

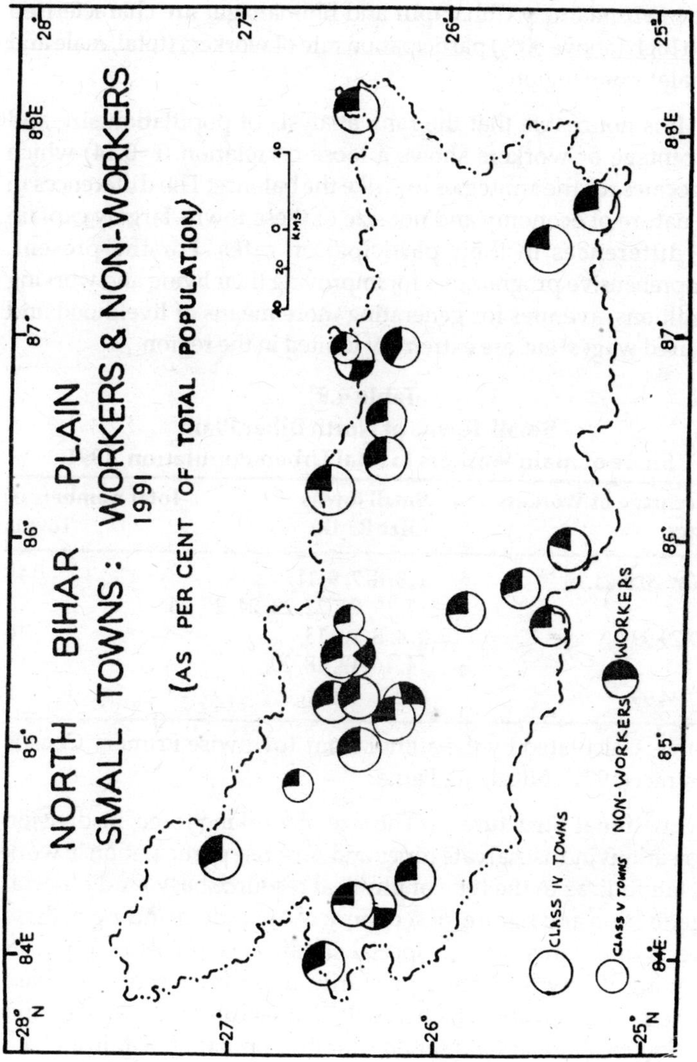
NORTH BIHAR PLAIN
SMALL TOWNS : WORKERS & NON-WORKERS
1991
(AS PER CENT OF TOTAL POPULATION)
KMS
CLASS IV TOWNS
CLASS V TOWNS
NON-WORKERS
WORKERS

Fig. 13

percentage group ranging between 20 and 25. Proportion of male main workers and female main workers is also below their respective average. In another ten towns have proportion of urban total, male and female workers (13, 14 & 16) above the regional average. Lastly two towns, namely Chhatapur and Bhimanagar are characterised with high (above 30%) participation rate of workers (total, male and female) in the region.

It is noticeable that the rank analysis of population size and percentage of workers shows a loose correlation (r=0.14) which advocates for the strategies to strike the balance. The differences in the nature of economy and not size of these towns largely explain the differences in their participation rates. For the present, comprehensive programmes for improving their living and working conditions, avenues for generating more means of livelihood and ensured wages, etc. are extremely limited in the region.

Table 4.9
Small Towns of North Bihar Plain
Share of main Workers to total Urban Population, 1991.

Percentage of Workers Range	Small towns (Size Rank)	Total numbers of Towns
Below 20.0-24.99	1, 3, 6, 7, 9, 11, 15, 19, 21, 22, 23, 24, 25, 26.	15
25.0-29.99	2, 4, 5, 10, 13, 14, 16, 17, 18, 20.	10
30.0-34.99	8, 27	2

Source: Calculated by the author from Townwise Primary Census Abstract (1991), NIC Unit, Patna.

Occupational Structure :— The size of working force, its division into various industrial categories and sex-wise participation in work are fair indicas to the type of physical resource basy kind of social organisation and nature of economy. : "An understanding of these aspects of an area holds a special significance for its man power planning"[19]. Towns depend primarily upon thier economic base framed by persuits which result in production, transfer and distribution of goods and services for the population within and out side the centre. The criterian, most customarily followed to decide the functional status of towns, takes the resource of percentage of workers engaged in industrial categories of census.

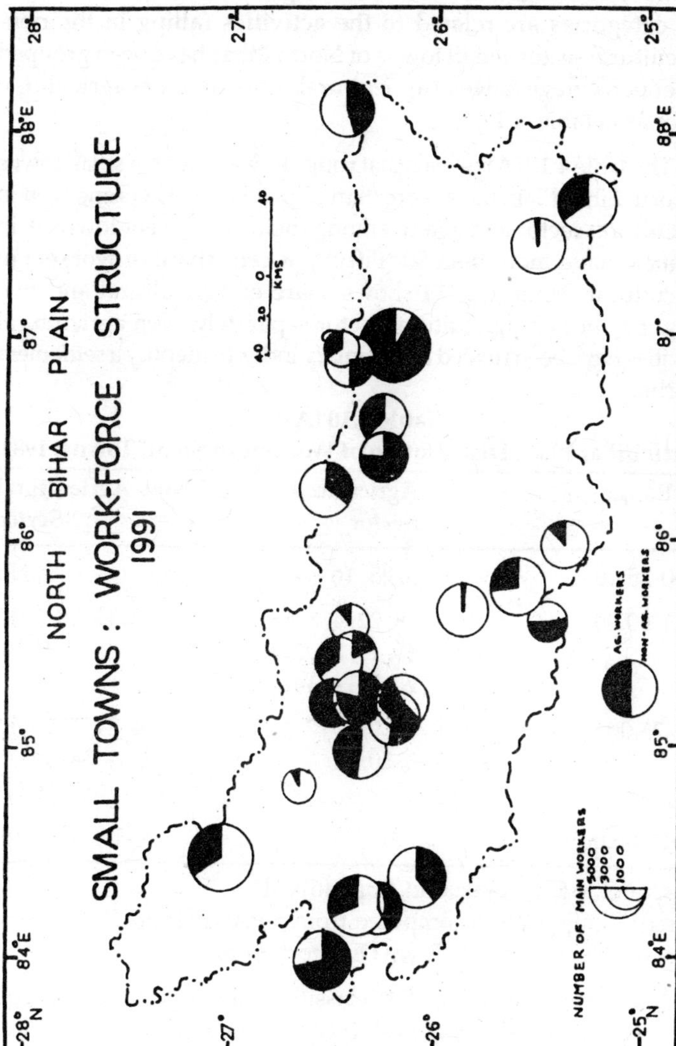
NORTH BIHAR PLAIN
SMALL TOWNS : WORK-FORCE STRUCTURE
1991
40 20 0 40
KMS
NUMBER OF MAIN WORKERS
5000
3000
1000
AG. WORKERS
NON-AG. WORKERS
28°N
27°
26°
25°N
84°E
85°
86°
87°
88°E

Fig. 14

Census of India, 1981 classified the workers in four categories, viz. cultivators, agricultural labours, persons engaged in house hold industry (Va) and other workers (III, IV, V (b), VI to IX). While the first two categories are related to agricultural sector, the other two categories are related to the activities falling in the non-agricultural sector. Small towns of North Bihar have been grouped under percentage range of agricultural sector and non-agricultural sector as in table. 4.10

The table 4.10 (A) reveals that roughly 70 percent of small towns of North Bihar Plain have more than 25 percent workers engaged in agricultural sector and again, among them 30 per cent towns (8 in number) have more than 50 (Fifty) per cent share of workers in agricultural sector. Fig. 14 shows share of agricultural and two categories of non-agricultural sector separately. Non-agricultural activities have been treated as a primary index to identify a settlement as urban.

Table 4.10 (A)*

North Bihar Plain Distribution of Workers in Small Towns, 1981

P.C. Range	Agricultural Sector	Non -Agricultural Sector
00.00-25.00	5, 25, 16	Nil
25.01-50.00	18, 22, 4, 8, 6, 15, 19, 21, 2, 12, 23, 7, 24, 14	3, 11, 20, 3, 17 1, 9, 10.
50.1-75.00	10, 9, 1, 17, 13 3, 20, 11	14, 24, 7, 23, 12 2, 21, 14, 19, 15 6, 8, 4, 22.
50.01-100.00	Nil	16, 25, 5, 19.

*Nos. refer to Size Rank as in Appendix-II
Source : Compiled and computed from census of India (1981): Series-4: Bihar, Part X-A: Town Directory, Patna.

The Census of India, 1991 classifies the working population into nine industrial categories of: (i) Cultivation, (ii) agricultural labour, (iii) live stalk, forestry, fishing hunting, plantation, orchards and allied/other activites , (iv) mining and quarrying, (Va) house hold industry, (vb) manufacturing other than house hold industry, (vi) Construction, (vii) trade & commerce, (viii) transportation, storage and communications and (ix) other services. In the present study two maps (No.14 and 15.) have been prepared in this connection, map. 14 has been prepared to classify the small towns in term of thier functions. Map 15. presents the spatial pattern of first ranking industrial categories of all small towns in the region.

Table 4.10 (B)*

North Bihar Plain Distribution of Workers in Small Towns, 1991

P.C. Range	Agricultural Sector	Non-Agricultural Sector
00.00-25.00	3, 19, 21, 22, 25, 26	8, 13, 18, 20
25.01-50.00	1, 2, 5, 6, 7, 9, 11, 12, 15, 16, 17, 24, 27,	4, 10, 14, 23,
50.1-75.00	4, 10, 14, 23, 3, 20, 11	1, 2, 5, 6, 7, 9, 11, 12, 15, 16, 17, 24, 27
75.01-100.00	8, 13, 18, 20	3, 19, 21, 22. 25, 26

* Nos. refer to size Rank as in Appendix-I

Source: Census of India, 1991: Town wise Primary Census Abstract, NIC Unit, Patna.

The technique used to classify small towns as mono. bi and multifunctional is the one followed by census of India where if a town engaged over 40 percent of its workers in a single activity is considered as mono functional [20]. The town which does not engage a minimum of 40 per cent of its workers in any single industrial category is termed as bi-functional, if the two industrial categories are able to account for atleast 60 percent of the working force all the remaining towns where no two industrial Categories are able to account for atleast 60 percent of the workers are termed as multi-functional.

The pattern of industrial activities carried on in different small towns in the region as revealed by maps (14. and 15.) brings to light the following salient features: (i) there are 13 small towns out of 27 under review which are mono-functional in nature, of which as many as 6 have the other services as their major functions. The mono-functions towns are old and they are more characteristics of less-

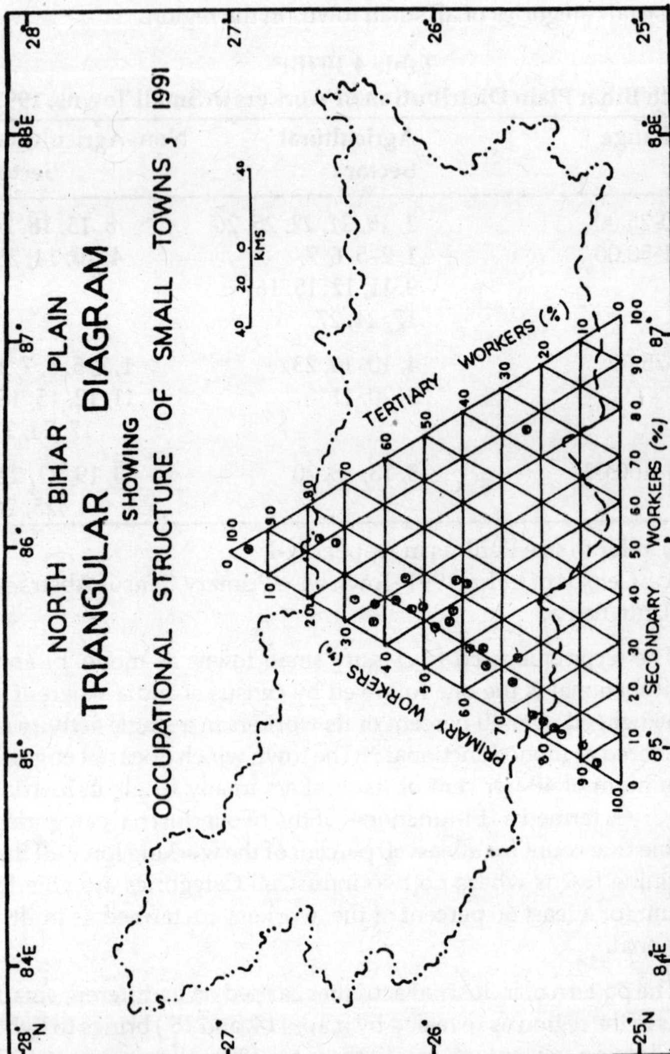
NORTH BIHAR PLAIN
TRIANGULAR DIAGRAM
SHOWING
OCCUPATIONAL STRUCTURE OF SMALL TOWNS, 1991
KMS
TERTIARY WORKERS (%)
PRIMARY WORKERS (%)
SECONDARY WORKERS (%)

Fig. 15

developed parts in the region. (ii) There are only three small towns which are bi-functional and have a combination of either services-trade and commerce or services-agricultural activities. Most of these bi-functional towns are confined more to agriculturally prosperous area in the northern part along Indo-Nepal border. (iii) The multi-functional status was earned by 11 small towns in which multi-functionality is confined : Services-trade and commerce-primary

Table 4.11
Small towns of North Bihar Plain : Their Functional Classification, 1991

Sl. No.	Functional Classification	Number of Towns
1.	Mono-functional	13
2.	Bi-functional	03
3.	Multi-functional	11
	Total	27

Table 4.12
Small Towns of North Bihar Plain : Their Occupational Structure, 1991

Sl.	Industrial Category	No.s of Small Towns having First ranking industrial category			Second ranking industiral category			Third ranking industiral category		
		P	M	F	P	M	F	P	M	F
I.	Cultivation	2	3	1	8	10	6	3	4	8
II.	Agricultural labour	9	8	15	5	6	3	6	8	3
iii.	Live stock/Forestry	0	0	0	0	0	01	0	0	0
iv.	Mining and Quarrying	0	0	0	1	00	1	0	0	3
v.a.	Manufacturing in house hold industry	1	1	0	1	0	2	2	1	1
b	Manufacturing in other than industry									
vi.	Construction	0	0	0	0	0	0	1	0	0
vii.	Trade & Commerce	9	8	0	3	3	5	7	5	5
viii.	Transport & Storage	0	2	0	2	1	1	0	1	1
ix.	Other Services	6	5	11	7	7	8	8	8	6
	Total	27	27	27	27	27	27	27	27	27

Source : Calculated by the author from Census of India (1991) Bihar: Town wise Primary Census Abstract, NIC Unit, Patna.

group or trade and commerce-industry-primary groups etc. Regionally speaking, the small towns of northern part in general display a greater deree of multiplicity of functions than the towns of southern part. This provides a fair degree of diversifications of economy in the region.

Further, the regional pattern of first ranking activities is simple with agricultural labour and trade and commerce claiming the first rank in 09 small towns each (Table 4.12) other services. .06 cultivation 02 and manufacturing (other than house hold) are the other important first ranking activities. It is only to be expected that the small towns in the midst of a backward agricultural region will have, by and large, agricultural labour as their first ranking activity. In the case of female workers agricultural labour is their first ranking occupation par excellence (15) and is closely followed by other service (11). The pattern of second ranking activity reveals that 08 small towns have cultivation, 7 other services, 5 agricultural labour and 3 trade and commerce. In a less developed and purely agricultural region like the study area where infrastructure for industrial development is yet at its infancy stage, a great majority of their small town towns possess an agricultural outlook and meet the primary need of the people. In the case of males and females patterns of second ranking activities broadly follow the general one.

The pattern of third ranking activities is rather complex with agricultural labour, trade and commerce and other services claiming third rank in 6, 7 and 8 small towns respectively, cultivation (03), manufacturing (02) and Construction (01) and the other third ranking industrial activities. Uni-functionality that too dominated by agricultural activities does not give a healthy trend.

All the above description show that small towns of North Bihar Plain, as a matter of fact, may be said to have failed in making a clear functional class. They have paucity of female workers and display monofunctionality and thus, are less dynamic in their demographic character. Again this shows how weak these towns industrially stand and thus, seek strategies for development. The unstable life of the small towns raises important research problems about their economic base and functioning of urban amenities which are the main tasks of the local-self government and need to be fully investigated.

References

1. Gandotra, M.M. and **Patel, N.L.** 1979 Economic structure of **cities and towns and their impact on urban growth of Gujarat State**". In place Small towns in India (ed.) R.L. singh & Rana, P.B. Singh, N.G. J.I. Varanasi, p. 145.
2. Clarke, John, I, 1972 **Population Geography**, Oxford, p.66.
3. Dayal, p. 1968 **India** in *Development Countries of the World* (ed.) S.P. Chatterjee, p. 347
4. Browning, H.L. 1961 "**Method for Describing the Age-Sex Structure of Cities**", in urban Research Method (ed.) J.P. Gibbs, p. 129.
5. Joshi, R.V. 1962 "**Urban structure in Western India**", Poona-A Sample Study, *G.R.I.* Vol. XIV, No.1, p. 8
6. Gosal, G.S. 1964: "**Literacy in India : An Interpretative Study in Rural Sociology**" Vol. 29. No. 3, P. 261
7. Davis, Kingsley & Casis Anna. 1961 "**Traits of the Urban and Rural Population of Latin America**", InGibbs., J.P. (ed) Urban Research Method p. 520.
8. Census of India 1991. **Bihar : Population Figures At a Glance,** p. 12
9. Davis, K. 1951 : "**The Population of India and Pakistan** ; Princeton University Press, p. 152.
10. Krishan, G. & Madhav Shyam 1978 "**Regional Aspects of Urban Rural Differential in Literacy in Inda, 1971, Journal of Developing Areas,** Vol. 3, pp. 11-21
11. Mallick, U.C. 1979 "**Development of Small Towns for Balanced Urbanization and economic Growth**" in place of small Towns in India (ed.) R.L. Singh & Rana P.B. Singh, N.G.S.I. Varanasi, p.65.
12. Smailes, A.E. 1953 "**The Geography of Towns**" Hutchinson's University Library, Hutchinson House, London, p. 41
13. Cippola, C.M. 1970 "**The Econoic History of World Population**" Penguin Books, p. 17.
14. Mayor, H. M. & Kohn, C.F. 1967 "**Readings in Urban Geography**" Central Book Depot, Allahabad, p. 85
15. Karimi, S.M. 1968 "**Functional Classification of Towns Bihar**

Plain" Trans. I.C.G., Vol. 5, p. 49

16. Singh, J. 1964 "**Transportation Geography of South Bihar**" Varanasi, p. 22
17. N.C.A.E.R. 1859 "**Techno-Economic Survey of Bihar**" New Delhi, p.Vi
18. Dayal, P. 1968 "**The Bihar Plain -A Regional Study,**" Trans., I.G.U. Vol. 5, p. 16.
19. **Krishan G. & Chandana, R. C.** 1971 "**Hariyana : Working Force and Its Occupational Structure**" Man Power, Journal, Vol. II, No.4, Jan-March, 1967, p. 56
20. Census of India 1991 : **General Population Totals** Part-II, A.

Chapter-V

Service Efficiency and Potentialities of Small Towns and its Impact on Regional Development

Geographers have been showing concern for problems of development and regional planning. As a part of the development strategy in a diffusedly densely populated country like ours, there can be no escape from a pattern of decentralization or dispersal of developmental activities if the benefits of socio-economic progress are sought to be brought to all parts of the country and to all sections of the society. Even in developed societies concentration is being supplemented with dispersed on ecological, social, economic and strategic grounds.

Our experience with the major centres of development has not been very satisfactory. While they have grown as foci of development their role as centres of diffusion of traits of modernisation has not been so effective. Within a few kilometres of every important centre or metropolitan area, one finds backwardness still persisting, giving the centres an appearance of island of development in an ocean of poverty. It does not, however, mean that there should be no centralisation of any developmental activity. On the other hand, whichever activities can stood the cost of dispersal and decentralisation should be brought to the small towns and villages. What actually required is that centralisation and dispersal have to be integrated in functional terms and a combination of aggregational and dispersal pattern of socio-economic development, therefore, will find favour in all closely settled developing lands.[1] Consequently, India in general and study area in particular, will have to think in terms of a further diversified, intensive agriculture and decentralised pattern of industrial development through an efficient system of growth centres.

There must be an integration and co-ordination of agricultural and industrial development so that each sector is complementary to the other. This has the potentialities of strengthening agriculture, agro based industries, labour intensive manufacturing works, electronic industry, engineering goods industries and the like. These should find place in small towns and service centres dispersed all over the region. However, the small nodes of industrial development should be functionally connected with industries in major towns and cities in the country.

Further, the construction of a close network of metalled roads and railways and the extension of electric power to every settlement, rural or urban, are necessary.

Attraction of service centres, no doubt, depends on its efficiency of concentration of services with its relative population size[2]. As Lloyd and Dicken[3] rightly pointed out, highest order goods being provided in a small number of widely spaced centres in functional hierarchy of scale continuum, service efficiency decides the varying ranks of centres. Hence, to chalk out an area development programme it is essential to identify the ranks of the various service centres and their service efficiency before hand.

It was with the promotion of the pilot research project in growth centres, sponsored by the government that a new approach to growth centres became widespread. These were referred to as the rural service centres.[4] The term service centre, referred mainly to a provision of necessary services for the rural sector, encompassing both the economic and social overheads. The project envisaged the provision of a whole range of services, including farm input provisions, marketing facilities, processing plants, repair services, local education, health schemes, etc. The entire emphasis in these exercises was on an 'efficient' provision of facilities. The efficiency was in terms mainly of minimizing the distances that people would assumedly travel to utilize these facilities. It was then assumed that these efficiently provided service will provide the necessary propulsive force which will transform the structure of rural economy. The socio -economic development of the surrounding regions of this service centre will assumedly takes place through improved agricultural practices, better utilization of the new service due to their increased physical accessibility. This idea of service centres planning has remained attractive in the most recent approaches towards regional planning.[5]

The objectives behind these different manifestations of service centres have thus varied from one to another. We may briefly recapitulate the major ones as:

(i) Spatial integration of both social and economic services to achieve:

(a) better supervision and management,

(b) better co-ordination and interaction amongst intersectional personnel and activities,

(c) minimization of resource inputs required for the provision of these services,

(d) an efficient transport network which minimizes the total travel distance (time) of people and goods, and

(e) enable villages to make multi-purpose trips.

(ii) Service centres as prime movers of development in the hinterland through :

(a) demonstration effects on both production and consumption practices,

(b) diffusion of new technology as well as necessary incentives to support it,

(c) development of centre into a viable urban centre and concomitant development of local non-farm employment, and

(d) mobilization of local skills, resources and initiatives through both the service provision and the above three provisions.

Further, in most of the cases, there has been some talk of linking these centres with a total hierarchic system of centres of different appropriate levels.

Identification of Service Centres:—It is important to identify the service centres in this region like North Bihar Plain. We first selected a package of minimum services keeping in mind the nature of planning process envisaged. The following general criteria were used for the selection of these services :

(i) Services which cater to a population beyond that of the settlement itself.

(ii) 'Policy' services that the government can take a direct action in organising these,

(iii) The costs of providing these services are within such limits that they can be provided throughout the region at each service centre.

(iv) In cases, like education and health were some standards have to relied upon, the existing situation must be considered and a realistic estimate made.

Based on the objectives listed above the following criteria emerged as the key one's for selection of service centres. Frequent visit to the service centre were deemed necessary atleast by the adult population. Further, as walking was considered to be most common mode of transportation, the limits of a maximum travel time of 90 minutes to the service centre was kept, which at an average rate is equivalent to a 6 kilometres distance. The second criteria related to the total population of the service area. This based on the discussions with the local developmental personnel was taken as 20,000. This limit on population size considered necessary to evolve a functional community. The next task was to select the settlements which seemed potential for development as service centres. A settlement was considered a potential one if:

(i) It was the peoples choice as a central place of a higher order.
(ii) It had a weekly hat,
(iii) It ranked high on the basis of centrality score,
(iv) It had high population growth rates,
(v) It had a large sector of non-agricultural, especially industrial activities.

With a view to evaluate these aspects of development strategy, an examination of service efficiency and potentiality of small towns together with emerging service centres in the region has been made in the pages that follows.

Measurement of Serviceability and Efficiency of Small Towns:

Present Approach and Methodology Adopted:— One of the important aspect of urban functions related to study of urban traits which may be dealt in three different ways, viz. (i) urban facilities, (ii) public utilities, and (iii) civic amenities. road traffic and electricity constitute urban facilities while educational institutions, hospitals, recreational and cultural facilities and banking facilities have been identified to constitute elements of public utilities. sewage, water supply, disposal of night soil and all such elements that create hygienic conditions have been included to compose civic services. These urban traits could meet the requirement of urban creativity as well as rural development. All these aspects of performance aspirations of small towns in the region under study have been examined in terms of their serviceability and efficiency. **Serviceability** refers not only to the number or availability of a particular service or services but to the nature and extent of their operational efficiency in relation with the quantitative and qualitative behaviour of people dwelling urban areas. The term 'efficiency' refers to mainly of minimizing the distances that people would assumedly travel to utilise these facilities. It is then assumed that these efficiently provided services will provide the necessary propulsive force which will transform the structure of rural economy.

The present measurement of service efficiency of small towns is based on exhaustive information gleaned from the reports and data published by the census of India, New Delhi. Altogether 24 variables grouped under 14 categories have been considered. As visualised earlier, the intrinsic quality of small towns is based upon serviceability and efficiency conditions and it is conditioned by a group of factors, viz. (i) inherent urban characteristics including road, electricity, educational, health and recreational facilities etc. and (ii) external urban features, like commodities export and import, financial institutions, distance from cities, etc.

In order to measure serviceability and efficiency of small towns in the area, above features of towns have logically been divided into three set of variables : (i) Primary factors which determine the intrinsic quality of small towns, (ii) secondary factors which influence serviceability and efficiency of small towns and (iii) limiting or negative factors which detract the quality or efficiency of towns. Each variable of the above factors is known as determinant of serviceability and efficiency and has been ranked according to its position and importance is ascertaining the efficiency.

Of the primary factors road facilities, electricity, education, health service and financial institutions are most important. Those together determine the serviceability in so far as they relate efficiency. They have therefore been given adequate score in an overall measurement. Among the secondary factors severage, disposal of night soil, water supply, nearest city, commodities exported/imported, recreational facilities, etc. have been considered. Among these factors relative importance of each individual determinant is less than a primary factor. They have, therefore been assigned lower score.

The association and ecological balance of the factors discussed above deem reasonable in maintaining efficiency of any town under study. From what has been made clear earlier this provides sound basis for assigning scores to different factors of serviceability and efficiency. This has been given in Appendix-IV for quick and comprehensive appraisal in the scheme of classification.

Studies of Selected Towns:— The detailed conditions of serviceability and efficiency of small towns obtaining in different parts of the region under study are best brought by an examination of civic and other amenities, medical, educational, recreational and cultural facilities together with trade, commerce and banking data. This has been done by making sample studies of eight small towns in the region. The North Bihar Plain is divisible in to four broad sub-divisions on the basis of physiography, soil and land use, economy and demography. The towns have been grouped into four stratified categories. Two small towns were selected from each of the categories on random sampling basis. The towns so chosen are shown in geographical sub-regions and some of their chief characteristics are incorporated in Appendix V.

The cumulative scores of primary as well as secondary factors for all the 8 selected towns were statistically grouped to find out : (i) Multi variable ranking co-efficient of serviceability, (ii) multivariate ranking co-efficient of centrality and (iii) gravity potential of ranking co-efficient. For this purpose, the following calculations were done to arrive of micro-regional variations:

Table 5.1
Small Towns of North Bihar Plain Multi Variate Ranking Co-Efficient of Serviceability, 1991.

Sl.	Sample Town	Rank	Aggregate score Ranking	Ranking co-efficient
1.	Janakpur Road	1	42	1.49
2.	Thakurganj	7	38	1.26
3.	Birpur	4	33	1.35
4.	Maharajganj	5	35	1.32
5.	Chakia	6	33	1.31
6.	Jainagar	3	43	1.40
7.	Dalsinghsarai	2	43	1.43
8.	Ghoghardiha	8	29	1.24
		V	24, C = 15 (cf Appendix-IV)	

Table 5.2
Small Towns of North Bihar Plain Multi Variate Ranking Co-Efficient of Centrality, 1991

Sl.No.	Sample Towns	Rank	Centrality of Services Aggregate Score Ranking	Ranking Coefficient
1.	Janakpur Road	3	12	1.31
2.	Thakurganj	5	16	1.20
3.	Birpur	4	12	1.31
4.	Maharajganj	7	9	1.15
5.	Chakia	8	8	1.06
6.	Jainagar	1	18	1.41
7.	Dalsingsarai	2	17	1.37
8.	Ghoghardiha	6	10	1.19
		V	= 11, C =8	

$$\text{Ranking Co-efficient} = \frac{\overline{r^1+r^2+r^3}}{N}$$

Where r = refer to rank of towns and
N refers to number of observations.
Variables : Refers to Appendix III.

Table 5.3
Small Towns of North Bihar Plain Gravity Potential and Ranking Co-Efficient, 1991

Sl. No.	Sample Towns	SC Score	Mean Ranking Co-efficient	Gravity potential
1.	Janakpur Road	54	1.90	9.33
2.	Thakurganj	54	1.73	11.26
3.	Birpur	45	1.83	8.80
4.	Mahrajganj	44	1.74	7.16
5.	Chakia	41	1.68	6.44
6.	Jainagar	61	1.91	12.69
7.	Dalsingsarai	60	1.40	12.18
8.	Ghoghardiha	39	1.71	12.64

i) Total No. of variables = 15
ii) Gravity Potential has been worked out

as in= $\frac{SCxCC}{SC+CC}$

Where SC refers to service score

CC refers to Centrality Score

iii) Mean Ranking Co-efficient = $\frac{N+1}{2}$

It appears from the above discussion that the serviceability and efficiency of towns under study differ. In the absence of proper infra-structural facilities small towns in the region exhibit insufficient performance. The index of centrality shows the overall ranking of the selected small towns in comparison of their ranking in population size. Relationships among utilities, population and area are dealt in terms of serviceability. Order of serviceability as compared to centrality is higher in Janakpur Road (Pupari), Maharajganj and Ghoghardiha while it is lower in Chakia and Jainagar. Variations in serviceability may be attributed to insufficient number and insufficient services. Extent of centrality and serviceability acts as the attraction for people by ensuring them services and establishment.

Measurement of the nature and extent of gravity potential is closely linked with the centrality and serviceability of the urban traits. It has been accepted as basic to development planning. Table 5.3 reveals that the potentiality of the available resources is generally positive, indicating their growth in active stage.

Potentialities of Small Towns:— In the light of the search of possibilities and limitations and outlined goals and policies, it was noticed that North Bihar Plain has variegated degree of potentiality and to grow ultimately to tell upon the prospect of small towns to develop. They, however, have their own chances to develop by virtue of their own potentiality to grow. They are, therefore, to comply with the call of development with different pace and different base of development.

It is likely that some places if helped according to their potential ultimately lead to the people's welfare. Any strategy attempting development must therefore gauge differentials in potentiality of these towns. A technique of five variables development potential gauge has been applied to group small towns of North Bihar Plain as under

An in-depth analysis reveals that towns fail to achieve any cohesive development potentiality and their ascendency with respect to any one variable is attributed to one special factor. Besides variables are not correlated, i.e. development in one variable leading to either

Table 5.4

FIVE VARIABLE VALUES CATEGORIES

Sl. No.	Degree	Population Growth Rate	%of Workers in Non-Agriculture Activities	% of V (a) Workers to total main Workers	Urban size Index	Service Scores
1.	Very High	100 and above	80 and Above	12 and Above	20 and Above	80and above
2.	High	75.0 99.99	60.0 79.99	9.0 11.99	150.0 19.99	60.0 79.99
3.	Moderate	50.0 74.99	40.0 59.99	6.0 8.99	10.0 14.99	40.0 59.99
4.	Low	25.0 49.99	20.0 39.99	3.0 5.99	5.0 9.99	20.0 39.99
5.	Very Low	Below 25.0	Below 20.0	Below 3.0	Below 5.0	Below 20.0

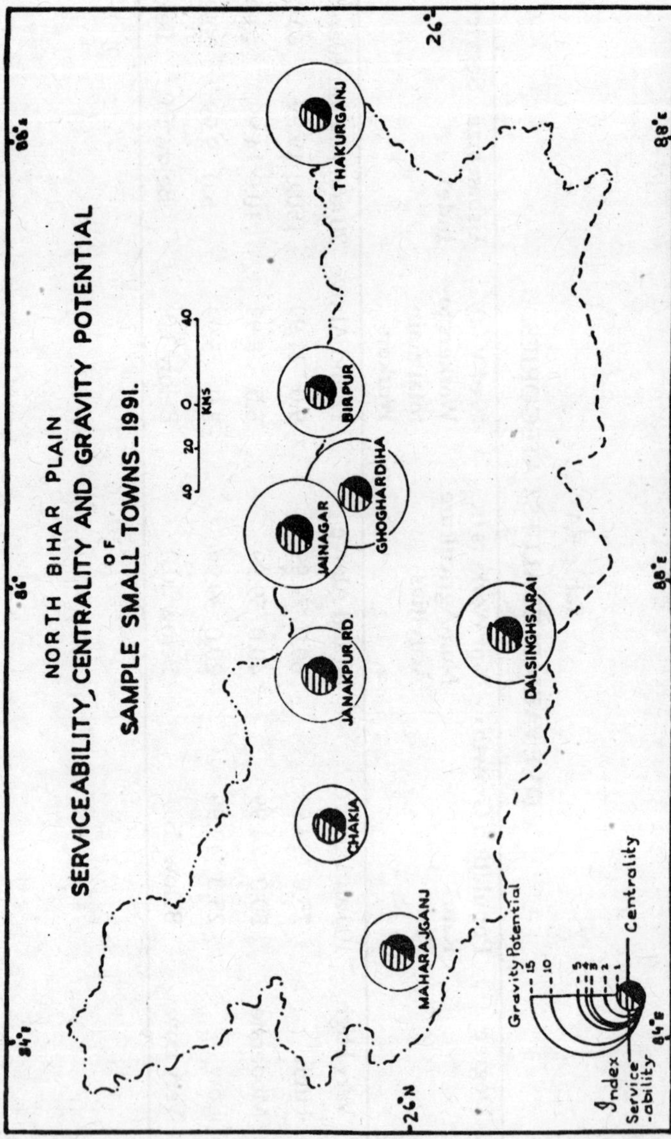
NORTH BIHAR PLAIN
SERVICEABILITY, CENTRALITY AND GRAVITY POTENTIAL
OF
SAMPLE SMALL TOWNS - 1991.
40 20 0 40
KMS
THAKURGANJ
BIRPUR
GHOGHARDIHA
JAINAGAR
JANAKPUR RD.
DALSINGHSARAI
CHAKIA
MAHARAJGANJ
Gravity Potential
15
10
5
4
3
2
1
Centrality
Index
Service
-ability
26°N
26°
84°E
86°
88°E

Fig. 16

lopsided development or to stagnancy after a few year of early growth.

The multi-variables potential grade of these towns are evident from fig. 16 & Table No. 5.4

Table 5.5
Development Potentials of Small Towns of the North Bihar

Degree	one Variable	Two Variable	Three Variable	Four Variable	Five Variable
Very High	6, 23 (A) 25 (B)	-	5 (B.D.E.)	-	-
High	4, 12 (C) 8, 13 (D) 2 (E)				
High	4, 6, 21 (B) 24, 25 (C) 1(D) 13, 10, 12,	7 (A..E.) 22 (BC) 2 (BD) 9, (E)16, 8 (BE)	18, 15, 14 (BDE)	19 (ABDE)	-
Medium	7, 10 (B) 8, 2, 5, 18 (C) 20 (D) 21, 6, 11, 22 (E)	14 (BC) 12, 9 (BD) 24 (BE)	1 (ABC) 23 (BCE)	- -	- -
Low	5, 14, 12 8 (A) 3 (B) 21, 19, 9 (C) 24, 23, 25 6 (D)	10, 16, 22(AD) 13 (BC) 17, 11 (BD) 20 (BE) 7 (CD)	-	-	-
Very Low	18, 2, 15 (A) 10, 1, 20, 17 16, 6, 11 (B) 4, 21 (C)	3 (AC)	-	-	-

Nos. refer to size rank of small towns as in Appendix I.

Towns of this region are almost equally distributed in categories of development potentials. But the majority of them shows their association with one or two variables, while no town of any part of the study area appears in five variable potentials category. One variable ascendency may not always be treated as indicative of very high development potential, because this situation is affected by some special factors.

The need, therefore, arises for a method to assess the individual towns development potentiality on the basis of effectiveness of all the significant growth variables. This has been done by working out development potentiality integrated Rating Index Formula, as adopted by Sharma[7] with partial modifications-

$$PIRI = N\ Pin_a \times Pin_b \times Pin_c \times Pin_d \times Pin_e$$

Where Pin = Proportionate Index Number
a, b, c, d, e = different factors
N = Number of factors (i.e. 5)

The selected factors are :

(a) Growth rate of population,
(b) Percentage of workers engaged in non-agricultural activities,
(c) Urban size index
(d) Service scores, and
(e) age of towns,

For each factor index number is obtained by making the highest value to equalise 100. In case of factor (e) towns existed in 1991 for the first time have been given 100 points but if they contain population below 15, 000 the point assigned to them are 90. Likewise, towns of 1981 are credited with points 80 and 70 on same basis. Towns emerging for the first time in 1971, 1961 and before 1961 have been given 60, 50 and 40 points respectively with a view that their long contemporary history simple signifies their stagnancy in terms of development potentiality. Proportionate index number for rest four factors has been obtained by getting the percentage of other effective index values to its highest value equalled to 100. The root of the multiplied value of Pin of all the factors, thus yield PIRI of small towns which have grouped under the value of range in table given below :

Table 5.6

Development Potentiality Integrating Rating Index of Small Towns of North Bihar Plain

1.	High (Above 50.0)	19, 25
2.	Moderate (40.0-49.99)	13, 9, 17, 24, 7, 12, 14, 15, 16, 5, 6, 10
3.	Low (Below 40.0)	21, 20, 18, 22, 11, 8, 2, 1,3, 23, 4.

Nos. refer to size rank of small towns as in Appendix-I.

PIRI values range identifies, therefore, a few towns in high range as developing once, a few more in the range of moderate as moderately developing ones and quite a sizable number of towns under low range as relegating or stagnating ones. The planning strategy envisages, therefore, not equal priority or concern to be attached to towns of all groups.

Spatial Distribution and Characteristics of Emerging Growth Points:—The emerging frontier of the spatial analysis have started from distance -measurement and ended at the modelling and generalization. In this process of initiation and result, large number of studies have appeared with special reference to settlement system. The fundamental concern in this reference is related with the relationship of point (p) and area (A) which are interpreted most frequently within two types of spatial vision-random and uniform, which are governed by the theories of poison probability and hexagonal net, respectively.[8] The early growth centre approaches, i.e. development of industrial and regional centres" revealed negligible impact in the hinterland. Studies by **Nair et,**[9] **Alagh**[10], **Mishra,**[11] make the point clear. Thereafter **Friedmann** and **Douglas** have put forth the concept of 'Agropolitan district"[12] which will supply the relevant services for the farm sector and provide off farm jobs. In contrast to this approach, the **Dantwala Committee Report** (1975)[13] identified the concept of service centres plans for the provision of infrastructure and generation of change.

Among the several approaches to the problems of urban and regional development the growth pole and growth centre policy is one. The purpose here is to indicate the extent to which this policy has been persued in India and the degree to which it has solved and can solve the spatial development problem of the area. The policy evaluates the impact of these policies on the spatial economy of the area and attempt to suggest a coherent growth pole and growth centre policy which might prove to be an effective instrument in solving India's ever growing urban and regional development problems.

The system of growth foci conceived here offers a strategy for plan implementation in the developing countries. The socio-economic changes in the society can be brought about through these foci, the national or regional plan on higher level growth foci working through the lower level growth foci, giving a new spatial organisation and order to all human activities.

Concept of Growth Foci:—

In the context of Indian conditions a four tier growth foci can be envisaged, [14] viz.

1. Service centres at the local level,
2. Growth points at the sub-regional level,
3. Growth centres at the regional level,
4. Growth poles at the national level.

Service Centres:— Service centres will be the lowest level centres of activity serving a population 5000 to 10,000 persons concentrated in one village or dispersed in a number of village and hamlets. The service centres will have grocery stores, general merchants, shops, minor repair facilities, tailor shops, barber shops, restaurants, primary and junior high school, a sub-post office, co-operatives, community centres and other basic facilities. It will also be the headquarters of an extension officer such as village level worker and other minor government functionaries. A service centre will not be a growth generating centre in the sense of the growth foci as described earlier more appropriately, it will be a focal point for social intercourse where the exchange of ideas will take place and from where developmental information will spread over to the village and hamlets. Such service centres have not yet emerged in India despite decades of planned efforts in this direction. So far, each revenue village has been treated as an independent entity and hence new facilities like co-operatives, schools and panchayats have been equitably distributed among them in uttar disregard to the capacity of these villages to support them. The time has now come to plan for service centres where these activities can be brought together to generate external and internal economies of scale.

A long term objective of service centres will be to create channels through which urban influence can penetrate the remotest parts of the country. The service centres would attract local talent to start an urbanisation process by way of diversifying the occupational base and starting a different style of life. The choice of the service centres will have to be so made that they strengthen the social interaction process and integrate the community served by them on a territorial rather than caste and class bases. Thus, they will be able to play the triple role for the regional development.

Growth Points:— The next level in the hierarchy constitute the growth points. For rural development purposes growth points will be crucial. These points will serve anywhere between ten to twenty service points. Each of these will be the focal points for a population ranging from 50,000 to 100,000. The size of growth points in terms of population will range from 10,000 to 50,000.

The concept of growth point as envisaged here is not very different from that of the market town in so far as the coverage and functions are concerned. The links between these so-called market towns and the villages are very feeble and invariably break down during the monsoon season. Most of these towns are parasitic in nature and function as local centres of exploitative collection of village products and labour for a few large towns at the apex of the urban system of the country.

The area under study, therefore, needs a perspective plan for growth point development to make at least the future development task easier. The growth points will be the sub-regional innovative and propulsive urban centres. They will be linked with sister growth points by state highways and with the service centres by district/ local road net works. The existence of a railway line will be advantageous, but by no means indispensable. The growth points will however be invariably connected to a railway line by state highway. In terms of service specialization growth points will be predominately agro-industrial. The most important economic activities at the growth points will be the production, handling and processing of agricultural and dairy products. In this study we indicate that smaller farmers are more livestock intensive, suggesting that dairy industry can play a very important role in solving the emerging agricultural unemployment problem as well as supplying of milk products in this region. If it succeeds, it will also solve the rural unemployment. The activities assigned to growth points should lead to social, economic and emotional integration of the respective Sub-regions served by them. Each growth point should have a police station, extension service centre, branch post office, banks, a permanent market place, ware housing, junior college, government as well as private depot handling agricultural inputs, especially fertilizers, pesticides and machines and repair shops capable of repairing tractors, lift pumps, strucks, cars, motor cycle etc. Each growth point must have a planning cell entrusted with the job of preparing development plans for the growth points as well as the region it serves. These plans will be integrated rural-urban development plans and will call for the re-orientation of our present study of development. Growth points may be identified for its tendencies to check the rural population to migrate into a larger city or interstate too for the employment.

Growth Centres :— Third stage of growth foci, may be described the development processes by the name of growth centres, which are not located in our study area. They will serve a population of 1000,000 to 20,00000 spread over a large region. Growth centres will have five to ten growth points within the area of their influence. Growth Centres are marked by the preponderance of secondary activities. It may be treated as even imagine a growth centre having the preponderance (in term of employment) of either primary or tertiary activities but such cases will be few and transitional. Such growth centres will be the consumers of finished and semi-finished products produced at the growth points and the agricultural products produced and offered by the service centres and the villages. One of the chief role of growth centres will be to function as countermagnets to the large urban centres of the country such as Kolkata, Mumbai, Delhi etc.

Growth Poles:— Finally, hierarchy of the concept of growth foci lasts at growth poles for the development of the region. Growth poles have a population ranging from 500, 000 to 2500,000. From a functional view point growth poles will have tertiary functions predominate over the secondary and primary functions. The growth pole hypothesis, in this way we find it useful rather indispensable for development planning at all spatial levels; regional and local. Growth pole offers a clear strategy for spatial planning and integrates the national, regional and local planning authorities to work towards a common goal even through functioning within their own jurisdictions. Unfortunately, we have no any growth poles in our study area of North Bihar plain.

Regional Implication of External Emerging Development Centres :— Urban centres constitute distinctive areas, which function as foci of general patterns of settlement. Dominating the pattern of the economic life, they are the portals of spatial interchange of goods connecting with region.

The analysis of various facts of urbanisation yields some relevant comprehensions which carry pertinent regional implication. Significant comprehension reveals that the "**greater rapidity of the urbanisation**"[15] forms one of the basic features of accelerated growth of population of the state as well as North Bihar Plain. The comprehension relate to recency, dominance, location and size scale behaviour of urbanisation which can be visualised as follows:

(i) Urbanisation in the state of Bihar is essentially recent one.

Current gains in its scale (5.40% in 1941, 9.99% in 1981, and 12.46% in 1991) characterise its recency,

(ii) The fact that urban growth is most conspicuous and predominant in the developing parts of the word,[16] also finds support in trends available in Bihar Plain districts which are fast tending to catch up with the southern plateau zones.

(iii) Successive size classes of urban centres tend to accumulate "**size scale**" with successively greater rapidity.

(iv) The dominant pattern of bunching of urban centres, creation of urban corridor, '**axial development**' and '**accretion**' has left permanent impression of the development of urban agglomerations.

(v) The 'twin process of outward extension and internal re-organisation',[17] deciding the growth of a town, has started gaining momentum,

(vi) The instances of sub-urban growth, metropolitan look, large scale urbanisation around large cities are now not varieties in spatial segments of the region.

(vii) The present spatial structure of urban development is not unwarranted. The process of urbanisation appears in no way "**an even process overtime and space.**"[18] The physicio- economic and socio-cultural situations are responsible for providing these distinctions.

(viii) By virtue of the possession of large population base and the impact of post-plan economic resurgence, the region may not spring a surprise towards the beginning of the 21st century if it holds the ace position among the urbanised states of India,[19] accomodating a greater share of its people in growing cities, multiplying towns and expanding urban industrial complexes.

Urbanisation being the function of increasing economic specialization and advancing technology, is based to implant the differential ordering occupation within a given territorial space by providing impetus to transference of agricultural communities into large non-agricultural communities. The trend, the process and the pattern of urbanisation recently found in Bihar bear the implications of urban and rural planning. Urban system has to be accepted to form the part of total rural settlement system. Size class implication of urban centres are to be obtained to "protect the old that we value and create the new that we want in principle". The protection as well as creation of small urban centres need special attention in planning strategy because these urban centres act as filter niche between the large urban centres and rural areas to facilitate the overall regional development, through urban-rural-nexus.

References

1. Gosal, G.S. 1980 "Frontiers of Geographic Research and Teaching in India". Presidential Address, **First NAGI Conference,** Chandigarh, pp. 4-5.
2. Brush and Ganthier 1964 Service centres and consumers trip studies on the Philadelphia metropolitan fringe, University of Chicago Press, Chicago, p.III.
3. Lloyd & Dicken 1972 "Location and Space : A Theoretical Approach to Economic Geography", p. 108.
4. Mehta, Meera 1982 Service centres for Area Planning Towards An Integrative Approach" IJRS, Vol. 14, No.-2, p. 175.
5. Kuklinski, A.R. 1971 Contribution to Regional Planning and Development, IPS, No.3, pp. 58-66.
6. Garg, B.B. 1972 "Optimum Density Patterns of Settlement in Relation to Environmental standards Economics of Development", **JITP,** pp. 27-33.
7. Sharma, N. 1978 Measurement of Unevenness in Distribution of Urban Population in Bihar : An Approach to Regionalization", **The North En. Geographer,** Vol. x, Nos. 1 & 2, p. 29.
8. Mishra, R.P. 1971 Growth Poles and Growth Centres in Urban & Regional Planning in India, **Journal of Development Studies,** No. 2, p. 19.
9. Nair, et. al. 1996 'Need New Policy Perspective in Regional Development' **Lok Udyog**' Vol. x, No. 5.
10. Alagh, A.K. 1973 Regional Planning for Industrial Aspects to Indian Economy, **IJRS**, Vol. 2.
11. Mishra, R.P. 1974 Urban and Regional Planning in India, A New Approach.
12. Friedmann, J & Douglas, M. 1976 Regional Planning and development : The Agropolitan Approach", in UCRD, Growth

Pole Strategy and Regional Development Planning Office.

13. Govt. of India 1976 Dantwala Committee Report on Block Development Planning.
14. Mishra, R.P. 1971 Op. Cit., p. 19.
15. U.N. 1969 Growth of the worlds Urban and Rural Population 1920-2000, **Population Studies, 44, Newyork**, p. 1.
16. Carter, H. 1982 The study of Urban Geography, Edward Arnold, p. 23.
17. Smails, A.E. 1953 'Geography of towns', Hutchingson University Library, London, p. 7.
18. Herbert, D.T. & Thomas, C.I. 1982 "Urban Geography : A First Approach' John Wiley & Sons, N.Y. et. al., p. 446.
19. Sharma, N. 1975 On on some Aspects of Urbanisation of Bihar, India, **Bhagalpur University, Journal** (Social Sciences), Vol. VIII, No. 3, p. 150.

Chapter-VI

Small Towns of North Bihar Plain : A Developmental Orientation

Town Oriented Resource Based Regional Planning:—The study of population consists of various elements such as its growth, geographical distribution and functions in response to utilization of resource in the economy of an area. The growth of population reflects its increasing-pressure upon land, the geographical distribution ranges from abodes of simple lay-out to complex and composite town scapes of multi-functional and crowded colonies of human beings.[1] Urbanisation as process exhibits many facts of growth essentially related to urban expansion and development of the human habitat but its problems can not be viewed unmitigated evil. Man's continuing efforts to adopt to his "system to society" and "space to economy[2]" to restore an ecological balance for human living and growth, necessitates that need for '**spatial**' and '**regional**' planning.

The demographic characteristics have their own importance in the study of the regional geography and a planning of a region. It is, indeed, through analysis of population features that an appreciation of regional differences can be fully made.[3] Man is a dynamic creature. His home, movement and field of activities are the primary bases of any geographical study. A few centrally sponsored scheme for integrated development would cover towns with a population of one lakh and below, on the basis of 1971 census. In selecting the towns for support, preference would be given to the town where district headquarters are located, followed by sub-divisional towns, **mandi** towns and other important growth centres. The district town or sub-divisional towns, etc. selected for priority development should be such as will check the migration of rural population to the large cities and would perform the role of services and market centres to the rural hinterland in the context of the balanced development of the whole district and the region. Another important factor would be linkage of employment generation with urban development and the capacity of institutions responsible for the urban development. As a space bound phenomena regional planning is not static but dynamic, a configuration produced by vast ecological process.[4] The theory of regionalism as advocated by **Francois Perraux** in terms of (i) homogeneity, (ii) Polarity or nodality and (iii) programming space: for practical purposes, could often represent one or a combination of these '**pure types**'.[5]

It is in the fitness of things that if small towns are integrated with their rural hinterlands and if they provide laboratories for innovation of thoughts and action, have immense scope for generation of employment and revolutionizing traditional agriculture into modern one. Further, possibilities for agrarian reforms, general consensus among the bulk of farmers to have the fruit of much publicised green revolution, application of manure and N.P.K. fertilizers as recent trends in farming technology and overall view of agrarian revolution as a continuing process for higher productivity from the land as basic to the socio-economic needs have to go a long way in increasing the inherent carrying capacity of the land.

India is basically rural and will remain so at least for a few decades to come. Under such a set-up, small towns scattered evenly in the vast rural panorama are certainly meant to serve the masses for long and better than the giant problem-ridden metropolises. But conversely and to our surprise, the role of small towns is being increasingly neutralized by hiatus between such centres on one side and cities on the other. Ecological organisation and social organization are the related aspects of human communities.[6] Thus, by assuming both the '**social**' and '**spatial**' objectives, one of the most important regional policies, therefore, resolves the conflicting claims of social profitability and economic profitability.

Since the ultimate aim of regional policy is the socio-economic advancement of the people, the main concern of development should not be based on the rate of economic price through which a given rate of growth could be achieved. Clearly, however, the scope of national development is wider than the rate of economic growth. But, nevertheless, it is the dimension of economic planning that provides a viable link between regional planning and national development. In India, to develop rural areas, it is necessary to create more small towns on a rural-urban continuum. This would remove the existing gap between large towns and small rural settlements. If a district is the unit of study, then whole district has to be viewed as a magnified shape of a metropolis wherein its residents live in various localities and avail themselves of facilities at the nearest market place but also traverse long distances for next higher order facilities, if they are not available at the nearby market place. In India, the concept of balanced regional philosophy grew out of its concern for:[7]

(i) growing regional disparities and unemployment,
(ii) demographic upsurge and urbanization
(iii) the growing congestion and urban sprawl of metropolitan cities and
(iv) polarisation of development and imbalance.

With reference to the above points, the state region of Bihar, possessed with a long hiatus in socio-economic history till the independence, display as an over all ununiformity in urban and economic development to-day. It is true that the vicious dimension of evils of excessive urban concentration is not the future of Bihar's cities, but a planning, following the maxim "**earlier the better**" with a notion to prevent the "**things from getting worse.....to make the better for future generation**"[8], deciding "how much urbanization where"? will aim at producing a healthy urban living and strong economic future for the state.

Through never an exact one, the science of planning by dealing with probabilities and tendencies based on past observations leads to guide and co-ordinate the future development of countries, and region as well as towns.[9] Planning is, however, a mental preparation for action,[10] but with certain prerequisites. It becomes, therefore, imperatative in present context, to comprehend the issues of "**why, what and how**"[11] or in other words, goal and policies applicable to the potentiality of towns and envisaged proposals, as development strategies for small towns in North Bihar Plain. They explain the essence that a complete plan is not only an utopian sketch rather they determine the process of execution as well.

Integrated Urban Planning with Regional Planning:—A country seeking development through planning incorporates into every new plan certain changes in the concept, methodology and content of planning. When the departure envisaged is substantial enough to involve structural changes in the politico-administrative set up of the region, it normally takes a long time for such changes to permeate the different levels and take operational roots. The goal of integration assumes in its essence, to combine urban planning with regional planing. The former refers to effective control over "Urban-rural ratio' the location, size, function and other characteristics of cities; the relation of the large cities to other".[12] Regional planning, on the other hand, is a means of development of communities adopted in size, distribution and occupation to the best possible use of land and other natural resources within their regions "towards an optimum of human productivity and habitability".[13] The goals, as pictured are, therefore, to comply with the "comprehensiveness",[14] of principles in India's planning, viz.

(i) Balanced development of regions,
(ii) Effectuation of maximum economic out put
(iii) Self sufficiency of regions to desired possibility and
(iv) Development of regional specialization.

There is a vital organic hierarchy between villages, small & medium towns and large towns and cities. The well developed agricultural regions of India have a number of small to medium **Mandi** towns in which agricultural surplus is marketed and the employment pattern is primarily of trading, transport and services. The big towns and cities, similarly are hubs for manufacturing and services. What is missing is that vital link between the small to medium towns and the larger cities. The focus of regional planning in the next two decades must be on the development of the small and medium towns and the developing linkages between the large and the small-medium towns. The task is clear. We need to use the latest technology, eg. Remote sensing, Geographical information System, etc. to evolve a comprehensive urban data base for rational, objective and people friendly urban and regional planning. To begin with the under noted steps should be followed which will then make regional and local planning much more objective and rational :

To Decentralise the Centralise Urbanization :— The tendency to concentrate regionally is high in the process of urban development in Bihar. The development of small towns has been aimed at decentralising this concentrated urbanization traits so as to have a "balanced and integrated region"[15] in Bihar.

To Check Disparities at Regional Scale :— There exists what may be termed as developed and poorly developed areas in North Bihar Plain in terms of urbanization, industrialization, income generation and over all socio-economic development levels. This is a violation of prosilient concept of "Balanced regional Development". An attempt has, therefore, been made to achieve a 'balance', 'equity' or near equity and "efficiency" in development processes through developing small towns in the form of tools bridging the gaps. This should cover the hinterland of the towns as well.

To Check the Trend of Hyper Urbanization : — Despite low level of urbanization, the majority of Bihar's towns and cities show controlled "hyper urbanization traits"[16] in which suburbanization spreading in to rural, typical of developed regions, deplorably lack. It is aimed to lesson the pull of hypercities and provide viable urban centres in rural surroundings by enhancing a local community identification and pride in living in or near towns.

To Transform A traditional Agricultural Region Into A Modern One:— North Bihar Plain stands basically for a traditional agricultural economy and rural community. Small towns supposed to be effective tools of dissemination of information, knowledge, and required inputs, have been aimed to be developed as real harbinzer of modernising agriculture, industrialization and economy and transforming rurality in to urbanity to a desired level. In precise terms, agricultural landscape in presently much different and more diversified form what it was a couple of decades ago.

To Integrate Spatially Separated Towns :— Several gaps exist in formal and functional hierarchy of urban centres in Bihar at meso to micro regional levels. The strategy acquires the purpose of bridging these gaps for which development of small towns will provide "efficiency of locational distribution of urban activities"[17] by integrating spatially separated urban centres.

To Control Excess Agglomerations :— The goal is also to provide an antithrust to the tendency of urban-industrial agglomerations near Begusarai sections and a positive thrust to achieve balanced regional development between large, medium size and small, industries on the one hand and between rural and urban areas on the other within a comprehensive regional frame work through developing method of techniques and organization to effectuate proper utilisation of indigenous resources.

To Accelerate the Industrial Development:— Industrial development, pinned as a means of "security, stability and higher standard of living "[18] and as the only hope of greatly increasing labour productivity levels of living, has been aimed to be accelerated in the planning strategy. Development of tea plantation in the eastern part of the region, specially over 1500 acres of undulating farmland in Kishanganj which are lying fallow, is likely to produce tea leaves worth crores every year. Besides, this will provide employment to atleast 50,000 people in nursery and plantation in tea gardens. Similarly, Jute industry and Mulbury culture particularly in the districts of Purnia, Katihar, Araria, Kishanganj and Saharsa districts will accelerate the pace of industrial development in the region. Small towns of the region will surely play a great role in this direction.

To Cultivate Habitability :— Urbanisation has not come as the phenomenon of unmixed blessings. Conditions of 'urban push back'[19] and thinning out of the population of village and small towns or atleast stagnation of these"[20] indicate towards the deteriorating state of "habitability",[21] have been associated with creation of larger cities. The present planning strategy ventures to cultivate habitability by extending easier and better access to the needs of villages and small towns on the one hand and by arresting the streams of emigrants to large cities on the other.

To Mobilise Resources :— If the resource mobilisation is linked to spatial planning it would contribute to the development of small towns and medium towns".[22] For removing the multi spherical regional disparities, to desired level, the present strategy aims to prepare a resource inventory of both habitable and non-habitable regions of the North Bihar Plain, in order to attain the national goals regarding mobilization of human and natural resources. The impressive gains of wheat technology were made possible in Punjab and Hariyana, thanks to the migrant labourers of Bihar, particularly from the region under study. There is something seriously wrong with us if others succeed in wearing our work force from our own fields and farm. Identification and protection of the interest of unorganised sector of large agricultural workers, therefore, are to be completed for the prosperity of the region. Proper laws governing agricultural workers should be enacted and made mandatory to protect he interests of unorganised workers. This will greatly enhance the agricultural productivity of the region.

Further, with a view to mobilising the vast water resources both surface and ground, required for raising the agricultural productivity level and to remove regional imbalances in irrigation, the state government shall partially open minor irrigation projects including lift irrigation for the private enterprise on "build-operate-maintain basis". The private organizations, in turn, would be allowed to recover expenditure by way of water cases and using the big chaurs, large governments tanks for **Makhana** cultivation, fisheries, tourism and forestry. Beside its cardinal role in the enhancement of agricultural productivity irrigation may serve the cause of social justice as well, by enabling the small and marginal peasants, enhance the land productivity through higher labour input required for intensive market gardening or dairy raising.

Small Towns Oriented Policy of Agricultural Planning :— The major urban policy issues involved in the management of urban affairs are that our urban centres are characterised as the poor and very weak economic and fiscal base with a low level of development and high spatial concentration of economic activities. But no matter whatever be the economic capacity of our towns and cities, political will is to achieve a high level of development, a reduction in regional and inter-regional disparities and on equitable distribution of level of living and productive assets for the welfare of the great mass of humanity. Policies must fix goals as to remove regional inequities through urban and regional planning. The North Bihar Plain comprises planning regions of varying nature as identified by Jha,[23] and the post plan endeavour of economic policy has set the pace of urbanization and industrialization a humble beginning. This will, however occur in harmony with the transformation of the agricultural-economic environment for development that has now set in motion at the Panchayat and block levels.

Apart from above mentioned policies, it is to be envisaged that the present strategy, the policy can not undermine the role of agriculture planning in present urban industrial economy. The countryside provides the avenue of surplus food supply to growing urban population, supplies of raw materials to processing and agro-based industries, of labour to work in factory of articles for export and therefore, agricultural development becomes the main content of regional planning.

The policy, further seeks the provision of the some of the basic community facilities, as a part planning for "habitability" and the procurement of development inputs, raw materials, labour, finance or capital and market if the adequate growth of small towns in the goal.

Proposals for Proper Agricultural and Rural Development:— Primary towns possess an agricultural outlook and meet the primary needs of the people. This group includes the industrial workers' categories I, IIand III which are related to farm land, the rural influence in the town and the labour force of various towns.[24]

Bihar, being one of the most ruralised and poorest states of the Indian union, must be given top priority in its agricultural and rural development, and this aspect must form the core element of any planning strategy. Most of the people of Bihar are scantily clothed, poorly housed, critically under nourished, diseased and largely illiterate. They are highly exploited. They inhabit the rural areas and link their fate with obsolete traditional agricultural of the State. They are in need of a patent amelioration. This alleviation is to be brought about through gradual change rather than changing it drastically.

Rural development should be a process by which rural people are to be enabled to become the makers of their own destiny. It should be a process of continuous growth and development of rural communities and their territories. It should aim at fullest possible utilization of all resources for and by the people. The objectives of rural development must embrace the avowed commitment to promoting both productivity and social justice, both generating mass employment as well as ensuring social equity, the overall goal should be to raise the quality of life in rural areas."[25]

Some of the general directives suggested for a qualitative approach, include organising for agricultural development in terms of efficient and timely production and distribution of the requisites of agricultural production, i.e. increasing their production, marketability, distribution and extension of production credit. Those for whom these directives have been suggested may ask for :

(i) Expansion of agricultural land by reclamation and extending immigration,
(ii) Intensification of agriculture by modern inputs and multiple cropping and
(iii) Mechanisation of the agriculture.

In case of land use, the scope for increase in share of net sown area does not remain much in plain in Bihar. as it is 69.33 per cent (1990-90) for North Bihar Plain, which varies from 56.5 per cent in

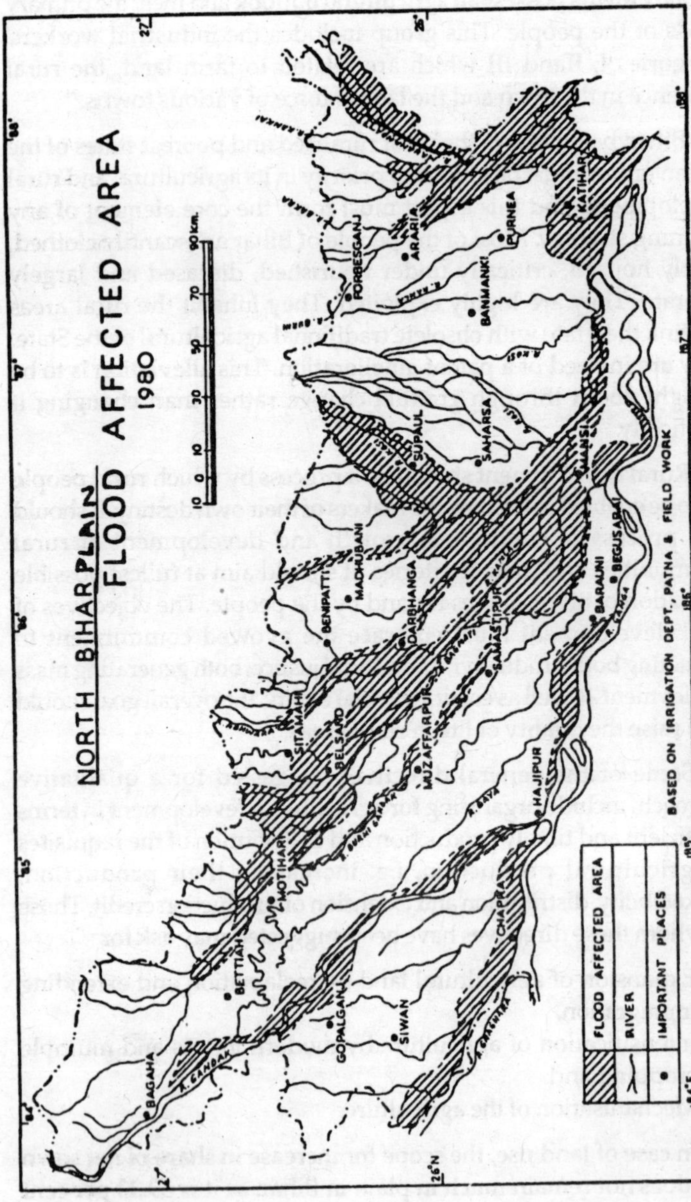
NORTH BIHAR PLAIN
FLOOD AFFECTED AREA
1980
10 0 10 30 50 70 90 km.
FLOOD AFFECTED AREA
RIVER
IMPORTANT PLACES
BASED ON IRRIGATION DEPT., PATNA & FIELD WORK
BAGAHA
BETTIAH
MOTIHARI
GOPALGANJ
SIWAN
CHAPRA
HAJIPUR
MUZAFFARPUR
BELSAND
SITAMARHI
BENIPATTI
MADHUBANI
DARBHANGA
SAMASTIPUR
BARAUNI
BEGUSARAI
SUPAUL
SAHARSA
MANSI
FORBESGANJ
ARARIA
BANMANKHI
PURNEA
KATIHAR

Fig. 17

Paschimi Champaran to 79.6 per cent, Purbi Champaran. It is noteworthy that thousand of years of continuous sedentary farming on account of favourable geographical conditions have combined to influence cultivation which has been extended to farthest limits. Not withstanding the fact, proportion of areas sown more than once to net sown area exceeds 50 only in a few districts of the area. This enhance the chances of intensification of agricultural output by bringing more and more land under multiple cropping. In the face of an ever-increasing population and their food needs multiple rather than single cropping system is gradually gaining momentum.

Considering the various controlling factors, the agricultural planning of the state region of Bihar should follow Roy's agro-climatic region".[26] He suggests a scientific method of agriculture planning on a regional basis because regional variables of cropping patterns establish the causal relationship governing ecological conditions and patterns of crops. The two most obvious problems facing North Bihar to-day are primarily to control flood havoc in the region, and secondly, to provide better irrigation facilities over a large areas in the state to counteract climatic vicissitudes. Further, what is more crucial to-day is innovation in science and technology of which some progressive and enthusiastic farmers are definely reaping the fruit-by adopting new agricultural strategies. Changes in regard to the development of infrastructure in farm technology, i.e. more abundant use of agricultural water supply, improved variety of high yielding strains inlieu of indigenous ones, potential use of both organic and inorganic manures and fertilizers and above all rural banking and credit facilities flowing from nationalised and cooperative banks are largely responsible for higher returns from the land now than what it was in the past. [27] Small towns in the region have increased role to play in this context.

Improvement in the productivity of agriculture is yet to respond as one of the most solid means of promoting industrialization and industrial development in the region. This emphasis is the need of "balanced development to increase Production in agriculture as well as in industry".[28] Keeping this in view, the proposal of development puts stress on the approach where industrial location will, specifically and essentially be proposed for small towns, the regions agricultural and rural economy and society are advocated to be reorganised and reconstructed by preparation of district development plans, regional development plans or any other viable regional territoarial development plans. These plans should lay stress on agricultural intensification, creation of labour intensive ovenues of activities, extension of education which will provide avenues towns with continuous flow of food, raw materials and human capital to the desired extent.

Proposal should perceptubly be that the lowest level primary service point will have collecting facilities of the agricultural surplus like milk, Makhana, fish, vegetables and grain purchase depot. The secondary development points should have some agro-processing beside the marketing facilities. It is incumbent to give a sharp thrust to development and to this end, it would be eminently useful to harness the energies and talents of the sons of the soil for the sake of bigger cause of the region.

Further, fashion show and catchy advertisements have become imperative for marketing goods produced by the rural craftsmen in the Indian and global market. Quality handicraft items produced in the countryside could not be sold too many times as the government departments shied away from doing their advertisements on the required scale and holding fashion shows. But arrangement of such fashion shows will promote sales of these goods by strucking the global buyers. For this, demand has to be created by doing market study and research and bring in innovation in designs of the traditional crafts of the rural craftsmen as according to the market demands. More particularly, innovating the designs of the jute made clothes and '**Mithila Paintings**", the demand of which is picking up fast in the world is challenging. For sheer sustenance of the rural crafts such business-like approach is the only recourse.

Proposals for Industrial Development :— Urbanization has been viewed inseparably related to industrialization. Urbanization, now a days, tends to follow industrialization. It is in this background that the strategies for development of small towns have been oriented to heavy reliance and emphatic advocacy for proposals of locating industries in these towns. This will greatly help in creation of effective job opportunities, generate employment and production and thereby will break to stagnancy and help these towns develop desirably.

A qualitative analysis of resource and demands at regional level shows good promise for the development of agro resource based and demand based industries in the region. It is in the fitness of things that small scale industries, according to several planners, have bigger employment potential than big industries and should be given preference. It is, therefore, proposed to put weightage to development of such unit in small towns of the region as far as possible.

Proposals for setting up specific industries at specific places need a wide range of qualitative and quantitative analysis in terms of their suitability. Proposals for establishment and development of various industries at different small towns have been made considering the following bases:

(i) Possibilities and limitation of physical and cultural conditions of the small towns with reference to man-space and environment,
(ii) Resource orientation of small towns at local and regional levels and the local and regional requirements. This should also consider existing patterns of important imported, exported and manufactured commodities of small towns in consideration.
(iii) Spacing, size class and characteristics of each small towns with reference to their respective district and their role in State's economic and planning regions.
(iv) Opportunity of employment and local resource utilization with a view to maximize profitability and over and above.
(v) Government policy of decentralization or concentrated decentralization with emphasis on the strict adhevance of code of work culture. etc.

Keeping in view above stated core points the author feels following proposals :

Chanpatia, Chakia, Lauthaha having at present sugar mills need improvement. Besides, they have the potentialities and demand for location of strew Board, Bone and Leather processing, Paultry farming, Electrical Accessories, Ready-made Garments, Fruit preservation, Steel furniture, Fertilizer and Chemical industries etc.

Mirganj, Maharajganj, Kataiya and Mairwa possess the potentialities for location and development of Gud and Sugar industry, Copper articles, Handloom industry, Rice mill, Paper Board, Saw dust Board, Bone-meal together with potasium nitrate manufacturing units.

Dalsingsarai and Mohiuddinnagar favour the location of resource based industries of cornflakes manufacturing, spices processing, paper making and modern Tannery respectively. Besides, they can provide best places for the development of Tobacco and

Cigarette industries and as demand based industries they favour the establishment of manufacturing centres of Agricultural machines, motor Repairing workshops, Medicines and Chemicals, footwears, Paper Boards, mixed fertilizers, Hardwares, Bone-meals, Ready-made garments, etc.

Kanti, Motipur, Belsand, Sheohar, Dumra and Rajopatti Talkhapur are proposed for the location of resource based industries of sugar, Leather, **Khadi**, Mustard oil and Pulse mills. These towns possess potentialities for the development of demand based industries of Brick-klin and Tiles, Rope, Agricultural and Electrical Equipment, Automobile parts, Surgical Cotton, L.P.G. Refilling plants, Medicines, Plastic goods, Aluminium Utencils, Distilled water for injection (Rajopatii), Candle, Fruits and vegetables conservation, etc.

Jainagar, Nirmali, Janakpur Road (Pupri), Ghoghardiha can favour the proposal for locating agro-based industries of Rice, Fisheries and **Makhana**, Mustard oil and possess potentialities for demand based industries of aluminium Utensils, Repair workshop, Agricultural machines, Handloom textiles, Furniture and Dairy products. Existing rice dal mills of above towns need improvement and modernization. A small scale steel plant should be set up at Jainagar. While Hume Pipe manufacturing at Janakpur Road (Pupri) may be preferred.[29]

Birpur, Manihari, Thakurganj and Bhimnagar have ample scope for the growth and development of agro-based industries of rope, Saw-dust Board, Rice, Cornflakes and Jute. The proposed cotton textile mill at Birpur-"The project town" needs immediate implementation. Mulbery culture may also be developed in these towns. Besides, among demand based industries Distilled Water, Agricultural machines, Automobile parts, Mixed fertilizers, Leather Footwear, Bicycle parts, Hosiery, Roofing Tiles, Hume Pipe, Soap, etc. may also be ' developed' which will help break the developmental stagnancy of these towns.

Katihar Railway colony, Samastipur Railway colony and Barauni Indian Oil Corporation, Township have great potential for the development of both resource-base and demand based industries. These centres have already a great number of existing industries like oil refinery, Fertilizers, Thermal Power, Milk Powder and Allied,

Sulphur, Glass, Acid, Special type paper etc. at Barauni-Begusarai industrial complex, Jute industry at Katihar and Samastipur (Muktapur) and Thakur paper mills at samastipur.

Besides these industries, they may also favour the location of forest based industries like Timber, Paper, Cane, Plywood, Matches at Katihar and Glass, paper and Ready-made Garments, etc. of Samastipur Railway Colony.

It is noticeable that the said proposals should be implemented as a time-bound industrial programme to ensure the planned development of these small towns which in turn, will generate employment opportunities and enhance the regional income. It needs reiteration that "Mahatma Gandhi Setu" over the river Ganga is going to foster industrial development in a belt extending from Hajipur through Sonepur to Muzaffarpur. This will give fillip to economic face-lift of the area.

Employment Generation :— Strategies and proposals will bring obvious changes in population characteristics, employment generation and their impact in the study area. Development proposals will open avenues for the job-creation for unemployed persons. Growth of small scale industries and handicraft in small towns will reduce the gap between employable population and the actually employed. This in turn, will push the participation ratio. Further changes will be noticed with respect to proportion of employment in different industrial sectors in two components of population : Urban and Rural.

Population projection of working force in the area, however, difficult a task, may be calculated through the survey. Estimation as related to the volume of workers within stipulated period of time becomes even more complex than population estimate. The only discourse left for projection of employment remains in taking the help of past ratios to total. What more can be done is to base the final results on some modest assumptions with regard to increased participation- ratios for the period to be projected. While projecting labour force, it has been considered that the adverse cumulative effect of intense demographic pressure, slow urbanization, low-non-agricultural employment, widespread rural underemployment will be effectively curtailed, development of small towns will bridge this gap effectively.

Man is a dynamic creature. His home, movement and field of activities are the primary bases of a geographical study.[30] The projected working population in the study region has been calculated below :

Table 6.1
Projected Rural and Urban Employment (in 000)

Region	Component	1991	2001
North Bihar Plain	Urban	754	1061
Rural	Rural	10012	11151
Bihar Total	Urban	3127	4391
Rural	Rural	21118	23755

The study area, thus, will record appreciable gain through net addition of workers during coming decades of 1991 and 2001. Increase in employment in urban areas will be exceedingly high in the study area. It is not only that there will be a rise in the volume of workers in total population rather noticeable changes in occupational distribution of workers will be experienced by this region within periods for which projection has been attempted. With intensification and growing modernisation of agriculture the well developed agricultural areas in the region will have a number of small to medium **Mandi** towns in which agricultural surplus is marketed. The employment pattern in them will be primarily of trading, transport and services.

Table 6.2
Projected Occupational Distribution of Workers
In percentage

Region	1991		2001	
	Ag. Sector	Non Ag. Sector	Ag. Sector	Non Ag. Sector
North Bihar Plain	83.03	16.97	80.79	19.21
Bihar Total	76.16	23.84	73.11	26.89

The change will be positive in case of non-agricultural sector of employment and negative with agricultural sector. This bears the impact of development proposal for effectuating the policy of deliberate urbanisation through stress on industrialization, Employment in medium industries as well as small scale industries will rise with prolific addition to their number as a result of proposals for their development in small towns of North Bihar Plain of Bihar

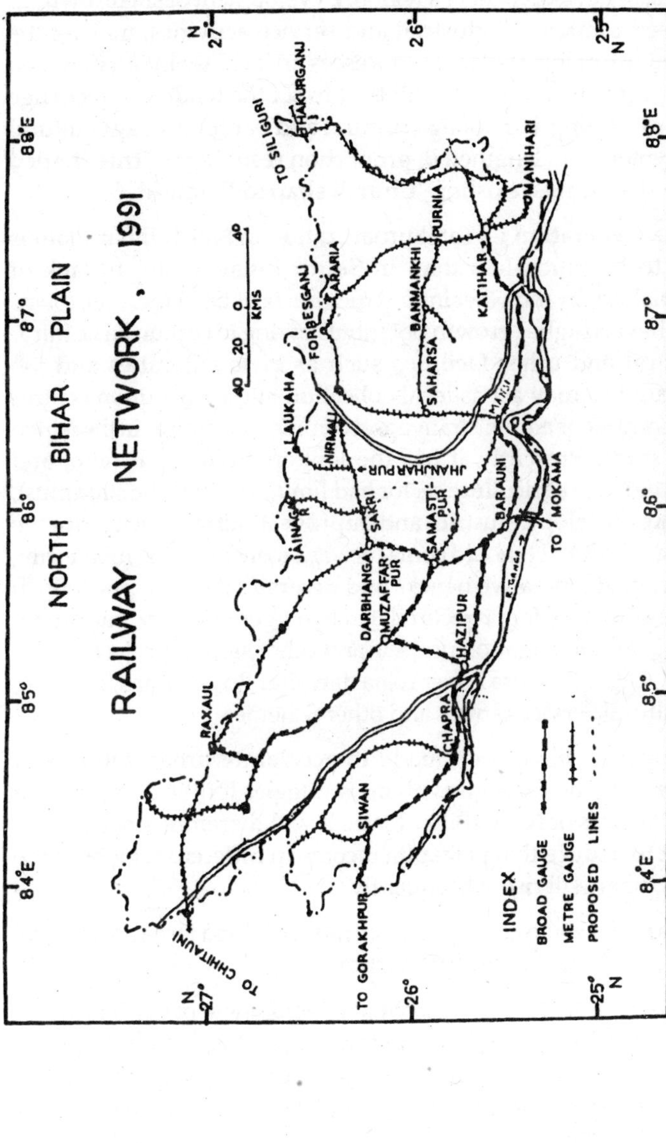
NORTH BIHAR PLAIN
RAILWAY NETWORK, 1991
INDEX
BROAD GAUGE
METRE GAUGE
PROPOSED LINES
KMS
40 20 0 40
TO CHHITAUNI
TO GORAKHPUR
TO SILIGURI
TO MOKAMA
RAXAUL
SIWAN
CHAPRA
HAZIPUR
MUZAFFAR-PUR
DARBHANGA
JAINAGAR
SAKRI
SAMASTI-PUR
BARAUNI
JHANJHARPUR
NIRMALI
LAUKAHA
FORBESGANJ
ARARIA
THAKURGANJ
SAHARSA
BANMANKHI
PURNIA
KATIHAR
MANIHARI
R. GANGA
KOSI
84°E
85°
86°
87°
88°E
27° N
26°
25° N

Fig. 18

State.

The projected employment indicates every possibility of change in "**occupation Pyramid**" which describes effectively, the type and the State of development of a region. Development of small towns as proposed centres of industrial and service activities, making the efficient use of local resources, foresees an increase in urbanization and industrialization. This will lead to set the tendency of change where exhibiting 'bar' for agricultural and bar for non-agricultural employment will lengthen in proportion resulting in "**true shaped pyramid** as against existing "**Church shaped Pyramid**"[31]

Income Generation :—Total urbanization in North Bihar Plain is likely to be much less than in South Bihar owing to lack of industrialization and other infra-structural facilities. However, towns which have a higher growth potentials owing to certain basic infra-structural and other facilities such as civic amenities and job opportunities may act as local collection and distribution centres service centres or administrative and commercial centres in the region under study. Presently, it has the low credit/deposit ratio, and advances to the agriculture sector had limited scope. The state must, therefore, develop industries and improve its infra-structure for the purpose. NABARD should come forward to increase the refinancing support of co-operative bancks and diversify the loan portfolio to include assistance for projects related to piggery, poultry, mushroom farming, minor irrigation projects and other similar projects under I.R.D.P., D.P.A.P. Indira Awas Yojna, Jawahar Rojgar Yojna, P.M.R.Y., Agricultural Service centres and other Schemes.

Proposals have been made to accelerate urbanization and industrialization through evolving strategies for the development of small towns of North Bihar Plain. It will therefore, not be out of context to deduce that percapita income in different regions of the state of Bihar will rise subsequently.

Share of income generation from industrial and tertiary economic activities will increase the proportion.

This leads to the conclusion that development of small towns of North Bihar Plain in response to strategies and proposals discussed earlier will bring enhanced income generation from manufacturing and service sectors which ultimately will raise per capita income in the study region.

Proposal for Linkage Development :—The proposed industrial urban development project was not an end in itself, it is also relevant for the phase attainment of agricultural economic resurgence which called for an integrated approach. Therefore, the linkages with the total development profile of the urban centres and the region should be clearly spelt out.

Given the appropriate importance and service inputs, some of these towns could absorb the dispersed small scale industries, along the population associated with them. Railways and Road assume great importance to the development of small towns as also to achieve maximum resource mobilization and utilization to assist regional development.

Proposals for development of rail linkages envisage steps : (i) to effectuate transverse lay out to bring diffusion, (ii) conversion of metre gauge into broad gauge, (iii) doubling of rail section to ease the movement and to optimise the region's resource utilization which, in turn, will help in translating industrial proposals for small towns in to excution.

New rail lines have been proposed to be constructed to connect seven unserved small towns in the first place and then to augment long range economic advancement as is evident from Fig. 18. in second phase. Small towns not on rail heads up to 10 kilometres, have been regarded as unserved by railway facilities. Name and distance of unserved small towns by railway from nearest railway station are evident from table 2.4 These towns should be linked by rail heads for their desired development.

Proposals for road linkage are : firstly, all small towns are proposed to be linked with road services and keeping in view the importance of road transport almost all the small towns in the region are proposed to be linked with district board roads, State Highways and National Highways. The improvement proposals should therefore undertake the following :—

(i) Provision of missing links,
(ii) Construction of major missing bridges,
(iii) Improvement of low grade sections,
(iv) reconstruction of submissible bridges with high level bridges,
(v) reconstruction of weak major bridges and minor calvents,
(vi) Construction of bypass for town and
(vii) Construction of fly over in lieu of level crossings.

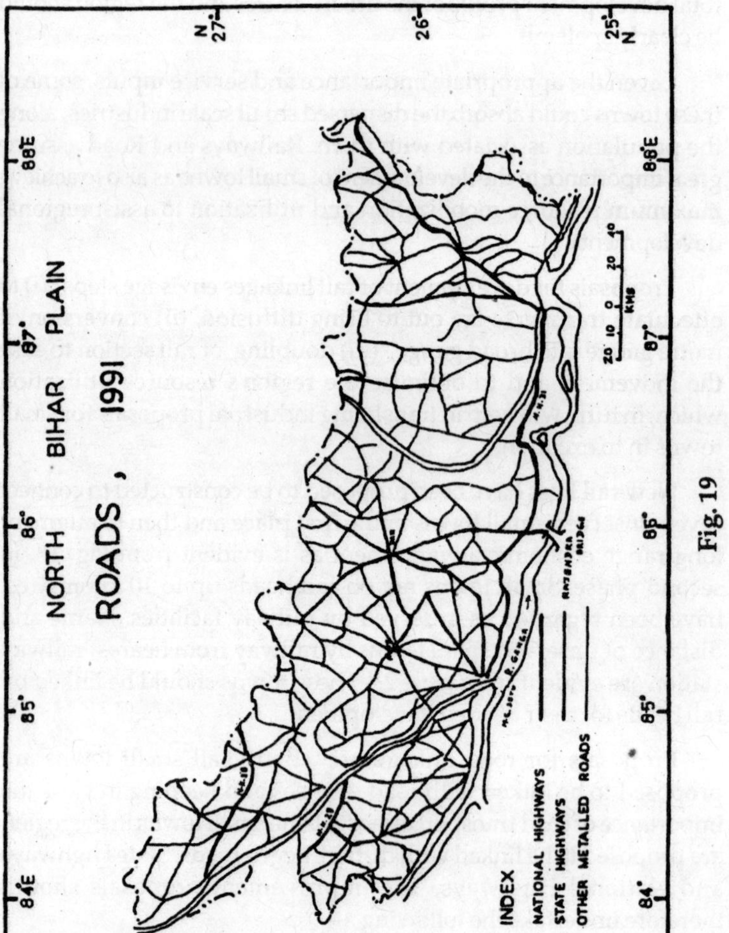
NORTH BIHAR PLAIN
ROADS, 1991
INDEX
NATIONAL HIGHWAYS
STATE HIGHWAYS
OTHER METALLED ROADS
20 10 0 20 40
KMS
R. GANGA
RAJENDRA BRIDGE
N.H. 31
N.H. 28
84°E
85°
86°
87°
88°E
27° N
26°
25° N

Fig. 19

Besides rail and linkages river like Gandak, Burhi Gandak, Kosi, Kamla-Balan, Bhutahi Balan should be proposed to provide better waterways, particularly during rains and serviceability for the regional development. Linkages planning, therefore, proposes to achieve maximum mobilization and utilization to assist town development and thereby regional prosperity.

Other facts of Town Oriented Resource Based Regional Planning.

The Indian society has a long tradition of rural life. It is, at present, passing through a traditional stage; and it has likewise experienced a relatively faster rate of urbanisation during the past few decades. Bihar, however, needs to be brought in central focus as it is the least urbanised among the Indian states.

The issue of urban regional planning has acquired universal dimension. It has emerged out of the developmental processes usually put the pace of acceleration with the application of modern technology. "The level of development, being largely a function of various physical, economic and socio-cultural ingredients, have been normally uneven in spatial dimension.

A significant index of development of small towns will be proportionate increase in employment and change in nature of sectoral composition of occupation. Secondary sector employment will go up. Tertiary sector employment will follow the suit. Present participation ratio falling mostly between 20 to 30 per cent will rise to range between 25 and 35 per cent as the generative proposals will unfailingly raise the level of participation ratio. It is equally true that percapita income remains higher in urban areas where productive economic activities are in the sector of industry, Commerce and services than the rural areas where sources of income has barely been agriculture. The kind of agriculture, practised in these areas in considerably consumption-prove and least generative in terms of saving and investment. Proposals for development of small towns aimed at industrialization and creation of job-opportunities in tertiary sector, may enhance the per capita income of towns. According to sources in the department of foreign trade, there is unlimited demand for Mangoes and Shahi litchies and all that is needed is scientific farming and good packaging. It is, therefore imperative that the region can profitably promote the packaging industry and small towns here have increased role to play in this direction.

Proposals lay stress on industrial development and seek reliance heavily on resource potentiality at sub-regional level of the region of 'North Bihar Plain'. Agriculture provides base for development in almost all the districts of North Bihar Plain. And the forest assumes significance in the district of Paschim Champaran. Small towns of Bihar as a result of development- proposals will emerge as growth centres on potential growth centres. They serve as growth points to form part of hierarchy of growth foci in Bihar. In recent years numerous countries have attempted to implement growth-centre or growth-area policies for the purposes of revitalizing depressed industrial areas. It is because these areas are by far in stagnant or ailing sectors. In order to stimulate economic development in such regions to come up to their advanced counterpart, this policy has proved its efficacy.

In may such cases, governments have also been trying to divert migration-streams away from large, congested cities. Despite its imperfections, growth centre theory atleast does offer the possibility of a fresh approach to problem of urban and regional development.

The government of India has also announced on June 3, 1988, its decision to set up 100 growth centres through out the country over the next five years or so.[31] Among them, 5 growth centres will be established in Bihar also. The following criteria shall be followed for the selection of the growth-centres:

(a) The growth centres shall be located in conformity with the distance criteria announced by the government, i.e. they shall not be within 50 kilometres, from the boundary of the 7 cities with a population 25 lakhs; 30 kilometres from the boundary of the 2 cities with a population of 15 lakh but below 25 lakhs and 15 kilometres from the boundary of the 12 cities with a population of 7.5 lakhs but below 15 lakhs.

(b) The growth centres shall be located close to district/Sub-Division/Block/ Taluk headquarters or developing urban centres.

(c) The growth centres shall have access to the following basic facilities:

(i) Proximity to Rail-heads, National or State Highways, if there is no such highway going nearby, the state government shall give a firm and time bound commitment for providing connections to such highways.

(ii) Proximity to adequate and dependable source of water supply.

(iii) Proximity to adequate and dependable source of power.

(iv) Access to tele-communication facilities, if such facilities are not already available. It should be ensured that the department of Telecommunication gives adequate priority to provide these facilities of their plan.

(v) Availability of responsible educational and health facilities, if there are no such facilities. In this respect the State Government should give a firm and time bound commitment to provide them.

(vi) As far as possible, the selection of growth centres should not lead to unprofitable divisions of fertile and available agriculture lands. Further-more, sufficient land should be available for the development of housing facilities and for promoting tertiary activities.

(vii) The growth centres should not be located in ecologically sensitive areas, so that denudation of the forests may be avoided. In sensitive areas, industries permitted by the Department of Environment shall alone be located.

(viii) The growth centres should be selected on the consideration that its sphere of influence would cover a radius of about 20-25 kilometres.

Small towns of Bihar have been given due weightage to the facts that they from the fundamental component of growth foci system in the State. They are supposed to contribute mostly to the formation of growth points in the broader hierarchy of "**growth pole-growth centre-growth point system**". It is, however, not always plausible to designate a particular urban centres in the name of a particular component of growth foci system for all time to come with a particular reference of a given region. The components of growth foci system behave to be ever changing. They, thus, produce the chances for the transfer of positions in the hierarhy. It is, however, rational to suggest the development of small towns as growth points in the existing urban hierarchy of the state. Big cities, a few in number and mostly spaced distantly, are considered to form the growth poles. Mediums size towns qualify to act as growth centres. The potentials for the growth as claimed by different sets of towns will, however, facilitate the chances for shifting of the hierarchy in the system. "The important thing is, therefore, to regulate the growth foci system growth through operational interweaving of urban centres of all classes to compose the components of the system."[32].

Integrated Development of Small Towns of North Bihar Plain :— All over the world, there has emerged a sea-change in the objective of development, especially during the last decade. National development which used to be assumed in terms of economic progress, has brought not just the benefit of a rise in national income but also many other problems which, however, neutralise the benefit of growth. This is seen glaringly in the demographic upsurge, migration to cities, shortage of housing, the problems of slums and squatters, the urban poor and those who face environment, health and sanitation hazards. Economic growth was not rapid enough to cope with the growing problems of a large mass of population. Public investment become exceedingly inadequate, the services and amenities-scanty, and the growth of slums and squatters unmanageable.[33] The road to prosperity at this crucial juncture culminated and took a turn to show that economic development is not always accompanied by social development.

Integrated development requires new approaches in the method of urban development including changes in the current status and methodology of urban planning and new modes of popular participation, including changes in the power structure that controls decision making. The plan, programmes and policies, affecting the mechanics of living, have to be integrated with a focus on a common set of objectives and a common approach to development. "We must live before we can live well" (Aristotle). The mechanics of living concern the conditions of human and material life. The art of living related to art of spiritual life, form of worship dance and song, but all these concepts of life, spiritual, cultural and artistic, can not go in a vacuum. It is essential, therefore, that we must provide the essential conditions of a livable life.

Since '**ends**' and '**means' of development are people** and their quality of life, the essence of integrated development strategy lies in "**operational explorations**" and "**linkages**" established while conceptualising the formulation of plan. This is the most important issue of integration. To make the programme more effective in its very intent and spirit, the issue of integration has to be conceived explicitly based on development priorities of town, in terms of integration of different goals and objectives directed to improve the quality of life of all people, beginning with the fulfilment of the basic needs of healthy living with dignity and social security.

This again requires integration of sectors and a wide variety of sectoral components of adequate food, shelter, income and employment generation and package of services like health, education, water supply, environmental sanitation including the disposal of solid waste, family limitation and protection against communicable diseases and aspect of prevention, that are more cost effective than the cure of diseases itself. This again requires multi level inter-sectoral convergence of services and their integration over space for all sections of population, particularly the most vulnerable, namely, the urban poor, the physically handicapped women and children. Bihar is one of the few states of India that has a framework of state politics for children, population and health directly relevant to the welfare of making in general and children and women, in particular. What is lacking is their effective integration at the grass root level of implementation. Partial efforts have been made in the past to inject the values and norms of integrated development in housing projects for the urban poor together with setting up of welfare boards for the welfare of unorganised sectors of labour force including construction, trade and commerce and agricultural activities.

Integrated development programme is an action oriented plan. It does not require elaborate plans to increase the ratio between resources as results. To make the programme more effective, the integration of shelter, services and infrastructure is necessary, in terms of following:—

(a) A single package with a view to minimising potential contradictions and trade-off within and among multiple objectives and using the achievements of each objective to further the cause of others;

(b) All the objectives must be given appropriate priority and pursued simultaneously; and

(c) These objectives must be used as the criteria for development performance and evaluation of results.

References

1. Singh, R.P.& Kumar, Anil 1970 Monograph of Bihar : A Geographical Study, Bharati Bhawan, Patna, p. 86

2. Wishwakarma, R.K. 1969 Dynamics Themes of Urban & Regional Systems Planning; **Arth Vijnan**, Vol. II, No.3, Sept. p. 359.

3. Trewartha, G.T. 1952 "A Case for Population Geography" **AAAG**, Vol. XIII, No.2, p. 87.
4. Wishwakarma, R.K. 1981 'Urban and Regional Planning Policy in India; Uppal Publishing House, New Delhi, p.66.
5. Mayor, J. 1963 'Regional Economics : A Survey, **American Economic Review**", March, p. 67.
6. Mukherjee, R.K. 1962 "Sociology of Urban Regions"; Ecology, Ervin Boskoff, New York, p. 68.
7. Wishwakarma, R.K. 1981 op. cit., p. 72.
8. Mclean, W.H. 1930 Regional and Town Planning; The Technical Press Ltd., London, p.4.
9. Mclean, W. H. 1930 op. cit., p. 1.
10. Glikson, A. 1953 Regional Planning and Development; Hague, p. 7.
11. Mishra, R.P. Sundaram, K.V. & Rao, V.L.S.P. 1974 Region Development Planning in India; Vikas Publishing House Ltd., New Delhi p. viii.
12. Peterson, W. 1962 On the Concept of Urbanization Planning, Population Review; Vol. 6, No.2, p. 17.
13. Glikson, A. 1953 op. cit.;, p. 17
14. Dutt, A.K. 1968 Some Lessons for Regional Planning in India; N.G.J.I., Vol. xiv, pt, 2-3, p. 162
15. Maciver, R.M.& Page, C.H. 1962 Society: An Introductory Analysis, Macmillan & Co., London, p. 343.
16. Bonifatieva, L.I. 1971 Problems of Urban Planning in India in Economic & Socio cultural Dimension of Regionalisation; Census Centanery Monograph, No. 7, New Delhi.
17. Hiresh, W.Z. 1973 Urban Economic Analysis, Mc Graw-Hill Book Co., New York, p. 293.
18. Bryce, M.D. 1960 Industrial Development Analysis; Mc Graw-Hill Book Co., New York, p.3.
19. Bose, A. 1966 Studies in India's Urbanization, Institute of Economic Growth, Delhi, p. 10.
20. Amiran, D.H.K. 1969 Regional Planning; Some Geographical Consideration of Objectives and Resources, I.J.R.S., Vol. I, No.2, p. 143

21. Glikson, A. 1953 op. cit., p. 8

22. Govt. of India 1984 Report of the Task Force Planning and Development of Small & Medium Towns and Cities, Vol. I, Ministry of Works and Housing, New Delhi, p. 90

23. Jha, T. 1984 "North Bihar : A Study in Regional Planning, "Approved Ph.D. Thesis, L.N.M.U., Darbhanga, Chapt. IX, pp. 256-98

    Also see Pathak, C.R. Aziz, A.and Chattopadhyay, R.N. 1970 "Identification of Planning Area in Three State Region", '**IJRS**', Vol. 2, No.1. pp. 64-99

24. Karimi, S.M. 1968 "Functional Classification Towns of Bihar Plain; Trans. ICG, Vol. 5, December, Patna, p. 49

25. Mukherjee, S. 1982 "Essays on Rural Development: UTSARAGO, Varanasi, p. 3

26. Roy, S.R. 1969 Agro Climatic Regions of Bihar in Essarys in Geography (ed. K.N. Das), pp. 106-107

27 Banager 1974 pp. 2-3

28. I.M.F. Report 1967 "Agriculture", Vol. III, U.S. Paper, Calcutta, p. 53.

29. Sharma, N. 1981 "Town Oriented Resources Based Strategy or Urban-Regional Planning for the State Region of Bihar, India", in Proceedings of the International Conference on Urban & Regional Change in Developing Countries, IIT,Kharagpur p. 107

30. Singh, V.N. 1986 "Spatial Urban Pattern and Growth of Urbanization", Inter India Publication, New Delhi, p. 78

31. Jha, S.N. 1989 "Small Towns of Bihar : A study in Urban Regional Planning Strategy", Approved Ph. D. Thesis, L.N.M.U. Darbhanga, p. 192

32. Hanson, N. 1971 "Intermediate Size Cities as Growth Centres", Prager Publisher, New York, p. 14

33. Employment News 1988 December, 10, New Delhi, p.2

34. Jha, S.N. 1989 op. cit., p. 186

35. Vishwakarma, R.K. 1982 "Integrated Development of Small and Medium Towns, (ed.) **IIPA**, New Delhi, p.5.

Chapter-VII
Conclusion

Summary of Chapter :— An attempt has been made in preceding chapters. (I to VI) to present a systematic and comprehensive approach toward population characteristics and the role of small towns in development planning of the North Bihar Plain. What follows here is a brief account of summary and main findings of the study so that strategies can be put forward to accelerate the pace of economic development in this backward agricultural region.

The two terms '**Urban**' and **Urbanization** as the fundamental elements of '**Urban Development**' signify the respective positions of scale and pace of a situation which has brought about a virtual transformation of the settlement history of population over the earth. The scale situation in this context refers to the extent. The scale situation in this context refers to the extent of proportion of inhabiting the form of settlement known as urban.

Size Classes of the towns are as follows :

Class of Towns	Size of Population
I	100,000 & above
II	50000 to 99999
III	20000 to 49999
IV	10000 to 19999
V	5000 to 9999
VI	Less than 5000

Altogether 27 urban centres (excluding the agglomeration units) of the North Bihar Plain which have less than 20,000 population, covering three lower categories of towns i.e. IV, V and VI classes are considered small towns and have been selected for the study. They play an important role in development planning of an area, specially agricultural region like ours. The importance and the need of the study lie for imparting integrated development of the economy of the region. The small towns are the most intimately integrated with the rural areas, providing them with most of the services and commodities, thus functioning as the lowest level of urban service centres.

Equally important is the role of small towns in providing stepped linkages in the chain of interactions between the rural areas and the higher order urban centres. All these, therefore, warrant a comprehensive picture so as to exhibit a meaningful study. In many respects North Bihar Plain is both '**Formal** 'and '**Functional**' in character. The study region in a viable space unit providing ample scope for assessing the role of small towns in the regional development in an admirable detail and has been chosen for analysis.

North Bihar Plain is a compact natural sub-region of the **Middle Ganga Plain** lying wholly to the north of the Ganga river. It extends from 25^0 14' North to 27^0 31' North latitudes and from 83^0 20' to 88^0 17' East longitudes.

It covers an area of about 53,798 km^2 with a total population of 39.2 million persons in 1991. Four administrative division fall within the study area. These are: Saran, Tirhut, Darbhanga and Kosi. Khagaria district under Munger division and Naugachchia sub-division of Bhagalpur Division also constitute part of the region under study. Altogether, there are twenty districts including one sub-division of Bhagalpur district.

With the exception of the Dun and the Someshwar hills in the extreme north-west, the region present an almost flat, monotonous and featureless alluvial topography. Though imperceptible, the general slope is gentle towards east and south. The region is the playground of many rivers like the Ganga, the Gandak, the Kosi, the Kamla, the Burhi Gandak, the Bagmati, the Mahananda, the Kamla-Balan, the Gogra, etc. whose fluvial action has to great extent shaped the socio-economic fabric of the peoples. The changing channels of most of these rivers exhibit conspicuous feature. The Kosi river for example has been steadily advancing towards the west and in the process, it has been lengthening its channel. Most of the lower basins of the rivers are flooded during the rainy seasons. The region has a sub-tropical climate with a seasonal rhythm characterised by a hot dry summer, warm moist rainy season and a cool and dry winter. Total rainfall varies between 125 and 200 centimetres.

North Bihar Plain is par excellence agricultural. Agriculture on the whole is primitive, basically subsistence in character whereby cereals predominate (73 per cent of T.S.A.), cash crops are subsidiary in importance and animal husbandry is worst managed. The cropping pattern that obtains in the area is diversified and a great variety of crops are grown among which raising of food crops is overwhelmingly important. Agriculture is intensive as much as the farmers fields are kept engaged throughout the year so that chance failure of one crop is largely compensated for by another particularly in the south of the region.

Being pre-eminently suited to ecological environment duly reinforced by a complete absence of mineral resources this region is industrially backward and undeveloped. The only medium scale industry consists of sugar and jute mills. Both are agro-based industries. Oil Refinery, Fertilizer Factory and Thermal Power Station are located at Barauni. Besides these industries paper mills, confectionary factory, engineering factory and rice-flour-oil mills are sparsely distributed in the area. Although the region is a flat plain, the development of transportation is inadequate. The railway lines and roads tend to run parallel to the rivers but not across the river courses. Metre Gauge Railway is still predominating in the region. Large areas are still without rail and mettaled road connections and their density is low.

Though the study region has a massive population base and an extremely high manland ratio, it stands a fairly low position (7.2 per cent) in the degree of urbanisation. Agriculture, the sole support of an overwhelming majority (over 90 per cent) of the rural masses in the region, is further symptomatic of stagnant economy. The regional economy is lopsided, inflexible and sluggish. It is in this context that small towns have got to perform a number of important roles in the overall development, with special reference to economic growth in the region.

A preliminary investigations has shown that out of 65 towns of all classes, 27 are considered as small towns in the region under study. In terms of percentage share in number they record 43 per cent of the total having only about 18 per cent of the total urban population. Most of the 27 small towns in the study region present a shabby look of unplanned growth and are therefore, slums and shanti towns. Naturally, qualitative aspect of their population give further a gloomy picture. They lack in employment opportunities and infrastructure inscntives. Further, spatial arrangements of these small towns indicate unbalanced, economic development as well as incoherent distribution of resources. Of late, there has been multiplication in the functions of these small towns, particularly to boost up agricultural production.

The inter-censal growth of urban population has been studied since 1901. The period of 1901-21 was marked by a decline in population. The growth was steady during the period of 1921-51, while it has been rapid during the period of 1951-91. There has been considerable urban growth during the last three decades.

Socio-economic characteristics of population of small towns of the region have been analysed in Chapter IV. High proportion of children (below 06 years) in their population represents for the most part, an economic unproductive segment and serious economic burden for the poor in an already stagnating urban economy. Small towns of the region have contrastingly low sex ratio than those of other categories of towns. Old small towns of the region display relatively high sex ratio while new small towns have deficiency of females. These towns are generally characterised with low level of literacy. Further, it is very poor in the towns where agriculture is the predominating activity and is relatively high to very high in the administrative-cum transport and manufacturing towns. Male-Female differential in literacy of these small towns further gives a meaningful picture in regional perspective. Differential indices have inverse relationship with urban literacy rates. Poverty and backwardness have been singled out as the factors of great significance to explain this patterns.

Workers participation and their structural characteristics represent the salient features of a regions economy. In the regional perspectives the small towns of North Bihar Plain reflects to very modest proportion of workers in their population. The main workers of the states economy 'lies in the poor agricultural base, which produce neither enough food for its rapidly growing population nor raw materials for its industry. The size of working force, its division in to various industrial categories and sex-wise participation in work are fair indices to the type of physical resource base, kind of social organisation and nature of economy. The pattern of industrial categories of these small towns reveal that most of them are mono-functional in nature. Bio-functional towns are confined more to agriculturally prosperous region and along the Indo-Nepal border.

Service efficiency and the potentiality of the small towns of the area has been considered in view of the measurement of services and facilities available in these towns. Micro-studies of some sample towns is also given for example. The multivariables potentiality and service efficiency of small towns along with the other relevant fact and problems have been studied and analysed. Proposals in the light of broad goal of balanced regional development have been made.

In spatial analysis, the regional impact of the urban centres vary from town to town depending on the size and the functions performed by them. Among the influencing factors of urban distribution, there are a few restraints to urban development in the region, viz., the uncertain nature of river, nature of soil, low-lying marshy lands, sewere and regular floods, parallel channels of the rivers from north to south, industrial backwardness and poor economy of the people. Subsequently, the last chapter elaborately discusses various facets of town oriented resource based regional planning, emerging pattern of small town of North Bihar Plain at a future date and also examines the strategies for planning proposals and indicates the direction in which these towns may be developed as centres of viable units of growth foci in the study region.

Main Findings:—We may now pass on to summarise the main findings in regard to the pertinent question raised earlier while dwelling upon the **Statement of the problem**" in **Introduction**.

(i) Physical environment as a stimulant for economic growth is at large highly condusive for agricultural development and consequent upon this, there is massive sustenance of a massive population.

(ii) Lack of essential infra-structured, non active participation of the people in the economic growth together with apathy of the state government are some of the basic constraints of economic development in the region. There are symptomatic of extant economic malaise and stagnant economy and constitute both cause and effect of rural backwardness.

(iii) The least urbanised, least industrialised and least developed region of North Bihar Plain needs an overall economic development in which rural and urban planning may be fruitful in the planning of various development ingredients of the region.

(iv) Small town is closely connected with rural development. These towns have great economic opportunities which, in turn, will absorb immigrants from rural areas and check the drain of emigrants destined to bigger cities of the state or elsewhere.

(v) During the course of population increment small towns of the previous decades have changed their size class. Further, the newly emerged administrative headquarters, viz., Community Development Block and Sub-division headquarters, market centres and roles of transport services may emerge as new small towns.

(vi) The emergence and sustained growth of small town is have the scope to create a viable settlement hierarchy to facilitate rural-urban continuum.

(vii) Small towns of the region are at present not resource oriented. However, in view of their high potentiality they might be treated growth centres.

(viii) The role of small towns in district planning context is also notable because they may facilitate the action of development as points of connection between district headquarters and large rural hinterlands.

(ix) The growth history of individual small towns reveals that no small town of the region under study has a constant growth characteristics. Their stagnant, slow or even negative growth show that they are very poor in their functional stand. The small towns have exhibited the most sluggish growth.

(x) Small towns of the region display monofunctionality and are less dynamic in their demographic character. These towns have weak industrial stand, low sex-ratio and varying rates of literacy signifying socio-econmic level of their people. Further, small towns of the region reflect to very modest proportion of work force.

(xi) Under the circumstances, the role of small towns in overall economic structure in the region is rather low. Even this low role and its areal variations do not show any close resemblance to spatial pattern of the economy.

(xii) However, spatio-temporal behaviour of small towns reveals that effective mobilization of various development ingredients (resources) in the region is sure to bring development of small towns which in turn, will utilize vast rural man power elicit their creativity and boost up economic progress.

(xiii)It is also noteworthy that small towns in the region have increased role to play in factoral development like agriculture, agro-based industries and building up of infra-structural components essential for economic reconstruction of the region.

(xiv)There is ample scope for development of industries utilizing the molasses for promising alcohal, food products, fruits and cash crops in addition to renovation of the existing sick mills of the region. Further, manufacturing units of leather tanning and leather goods, bone crushing mills, manufacturing of agricultural implements such as improved ploughs, threshers, etc. can easily be taken up in small towns throughout the region. This will give fillip to economic face-lift of the area.

Strategy for development :—For economic reconstruction and resource-based urban regional planning of the North Bihar Plain detailed strategies have been put forth in the preceding chapter (vi). However, the following points are worthy to mention:

(i) For economic progress and operationalisation of integrated rural-urban development the policy makers and planner must conceive small towns as an instrument for quickening the rate of growth and development and transformation.

(ii) Instead of treating urbanisation as a process of working against rural development, it should be viewed as means to develop rural areas.

(iii) The provision of various social, educational and health services, which are currently located at far off places, needs to be located at such centres which are accessible to the users within reasonable travel distance.

(iv) To comply with the comprehensiveness of principles in India's planning" as decent in 6.2 of this book, the focus of regional planning must be on the development of small and market towns and developing linkages between the large and small medium towns.

(v) Development of small towns aimed at small scale industrialisation and creation of job opportunities in tertiary sector, may rise the per capita income of towns.

(vi) Small towns oriented policy of agricultural planning will transform the agricultural-economic environment for development that has now set in motion at the Panchayat and Block levels, etc.

Finally, what is needed therefore is to bring developmental thrust in the region. If various measures as outlines above are carried with vigour and sincerity, there seems to be no reason why sluggish economy of the region is not accelerated. Some such changes-economic, social and institutional are surely around the corner in the study region.

Chapter-VIII

Regional Population : Contemporary Directions

The bifurcation of the state of Bihar into Bihar and Jharkhand on November 15, 2000 has its obvious impact on pace and degree of urbanization in the state of present Bihar, Bihar continues to stand as one of the least urbanized part of the country. According to 2001 census, only 10.47 per cent of its total population is classified as urban which roughly tallies with 1991 figure of 10.40 percent. The state of Bihar, thus continues to be predominantly rural in character with over whelming high proportion of 89.53 percent of rural population. The picture of North Bihar Plain is even more desired as only 6.8 percent of its total population live in towns of various size in 2001, further, only 12 out of a total number's of 68 town in the region are classified as small towns.

The region under study covers an area of about 53,798 sq kms and has a population of about 51.74 million, with a density of about 1001 persons per sq kms according to 2001 census. However, number of small towns in the region has drastically declined from 27 in 1991 to mere 12 in 2001. A large number of small towns of 1991 have either been up graded to class III towns or merged with neighbouring towns as urban agglomeration and even some have been declassified. Evidently its dubious connotation of being one of the ôleast urbanizedö least industrialized and ôleast developedö among the states of the union of India. Strongly persists even at the dawn of the 21st century. The regional economy continues to be lopsided (agricultural), inflexible and sluggish. It is in this context that small towns bear significance with special reference to economic growth in the region.

Declining number of small towns in 2001 their widespread location in the region and possible propensity to grow are supposed to provide the area viable base to effectuate the most desired balanced urban regional growth. Some salient features of small towns of 2001 in the region discernable from the tables given below:-

Table 8.1
North Bihar Plain : District wise Urban Population, Literacy & Occupational Structure- 2001

S.No.	District	No. of City/Towns	Urban Pop. As % of Total Pop.	Literacy			Occupational Structure In %		
				Total	Rural	Urban	Primary sector	Secondary sector	Tertiary sector
1	2	3	4	5	6	7	8	9	10
1	Paschim Champaran	5	9.16	36.63	36.31	64.50	83.60	2.68	13.74
2	Purbi Champaran	7	6.16	38.14	35.99	68.29	82.15	2.73	15.12
3	Sheohar	1	4.17	37.01	36.71	43.93	87.48	2.28	10.30
4	Sitamarhi	5	6.61	39.38	37.63	66.96	79.23	3.26	15.51
5	Madhubani	4	4.48	42.35	41.55	63.69	86.37	3.33	13.30
6	Supaul	3	6.24	37.80	36.57	59.87	88.84	2.40	8.76
7	Araria	3	6.24	34.94	33.07	61.70	88.11	1.83	10.06
8	Kishanganj	3	9.16	31.02	27.68	59.71	84.23	1.93	13.84
9	Purnea	3	8.74	35.51	31.80	71.85	86.0	2.00	12.00
10	Katihar	3	9.11	35.29	31.19	73.03	83.52	2.12	14.36
11	Madhepura	2	4.14	36.19	34.64	67.36	89.61	1.74	8.65
12	Saharsa	1	8.23	39.28	36.340	69.93	84.13	2.05	13.82
13	Darbhanga	1	8.12	44.32	41.39	75.63	73.94	4.09	21.97

14	Muzaffarpur	3	9.30	48.15	44.87	78.04	71.07	3.28	25.65
15	Gopalganj	A	6.17	48.19	47.19	63.25	79.46	4.52	16.62
16	Siwan	3	5.15	52.01	50.86	70.98	75.41	3.86	22.81
17	Saran	5	9.17	52.01	50.43	67.01	73.33	4.02	23.23
18	Vaishali	3	6.88	51.63	50.50	66.54	72.75	4.02	23.23
19	Samastipur	4	6.62	45.76	44.55	76.40	75.58	4.12	30.30
20	Begusarai	2	4.12	48.55	47.01	78.79	66.48	7.06	26.46
21	Khagaria	2	5.97	41.56	39.67	70.14	80.39	2.49	17.12
22	Naugachia (part. of Bhagalpur)	1	4.13	47.70	42.75	58.60	78.20	5.30	11.28
	North Bihar Plain	68	6.8	39.68	37.02	62.16	80.55	3.13	17.05

Source : Census of India-2001, Bihar, Provisional Total

Table 8.2
Bihar Trends of Urbanization 1901-2001

Census Year	Total Nos. of Uas/TGS Towns	Population Size	Total Urban Population	Percent Urban Population	Decennial Growth Absolute	Percent	Annual Exponential Growth Rate (Urban)
1	2	3	4	5	6	7	8
1901	44	21243632	979010	4.61	-	-	-
1911	43	21567159	919059	4.26	-59951	-6.12	-0.63
1921	46	21358905	921915	4.32	-2856	+0.31	0.03
1931	48	23438371	1099896	4.69	177981	+19.31	1.77
1941	58	26302771	1392850	5.30	292954	+26.63	2.36
1951	73	29085017	1865911	6.42	473061	+33.96	2.92
1961	(6 TGA) 88	34840968	2580578	7.41	714667	+38.30	3.24
1971	(7 UAS) 106	42126236	3356334	7.97	775756	+30.06	2.63
1981	(7 UAS) 119	52302665	5144945	9.84	1788611	+153.29	4.27
1991	(7 UAS) 138	64530554	6711785	10.40	1566840	+30.45	2.66
2001	(7 UAS) 130	82878796	8679200	1047	1967415	+29.31	2.57

Source : Computed from Census of India, 2001, Provisional Population Total.

Table 8.3

North Bihar Plain : GROWTH INDICES OF SMALL TOWNS- 1901 û2001

Years	No. of Small Towns	Total Population of Small Towns	Growth Indices
1	2	3	4
1901	3	31445	100.0
1911	3	25386	80.73
1921	3	21448	68.21
1931	3	24639	78.36
1941	4	28482	90.58
1951	8	73038	232.27
1961	14	137863	526.48
1971	17	196997	554.71
1981	25	366143	1064.18
1991	27	379826	1107.91
2001	12	186915	594.42

Source : Compiled from Census of India (1981) Series 4, Bihar, Towns Directory, Part-XA; Town-wise Primary Census, Abstract, 1991- and Provisional Population Totals, Paper 2 of 2001.

Table 8.4 (A)
Population Characteristic of Small Towns of North Bihar - 2001

Sl. No.	Name	Status	Population Size Total	Male	Female	Growth Rate (%) 1991-2001	Persons Per KM^2	Sex Ratio	Literacy T	M	F
1	2	3	4	5	6	7	8	9	10	11	12
1	Jainagar	N.A.	19493	10343	9150	14.81	12576.1	885	69.54	80.30	57.35
2	Mairwa	N.A.	18696	9834	8862	22.88	3000.9	901	64.83	76.94	51.23
3	Katiya	N.A.	17896	9284	8612	34.19	1607.9	928	51.63	65.30	36.92
4	Belsand	N.A.	17821	9511	8310	25.93	1766.2	874	41.45	50.48	30.89
5	Birpur	N.A.	17730	9495	8235	20.27	2044.9	867	66.45	77.84	53.72
6	Chakia	N.A.	16618	8868	7750	21.23	267.4	874	61.56	72.53	49.02
7	Nirmali	N.A.	16144	8521	7623	17.13	3046.0	895	54.40	68.44	38.39
8	Thakurganj	N.A.	15288	8075	7213	12.50	1461.5	893	64.97	75.04	53.59
9	Ghoghardiha	N.A.	14523	7474	7049	2082	1663.5	943	52.58	64.50	39.90
10	Mohiuddinnagar	N.A.	13764	7136	6628	24.99	1703.4	829	55.57	66.09	44.32
11	Janakpur Rd.	N.A.	13341	7114	6227	39.11	4303.5	875	77.15	86.73	66.26
12	Raghunathpur	CT	5601	3054	2547	-	1672.6	834	64.91	74.27	53.25

Table 8.4 (B)
List of Towns of 1991, declassified / Merged with Other Towns in 2001

Sl. No.	Name of Town	Name of District	Population Size in 1991
1.	Chhatapur	Supaul	16746
2.	Bhimnagar (CT)	Supaul	5673
3.	Barauni (CT)	Begusarai	60685
4.	Teghra (CT)	Begusarai	32999
5.	Bihariganj (CT)	Madhepura	23452
6.	Hassanpur (CT)	Samastipur	23941

The recent trend of urbanization in the region shows sharp decline in absolute size as well as number of small towns leading to hierarchical imbalance in size distribution of urban centres. Indeed it is very disappointing that number of small towns are declining. Details of the growth indices are evident from the table III

Table IV shows changes in social indices like literacy rate and male female differentials in literacy of present small towns of the North Bihar Plain. Among 12 small towns of the region Jainagar recorded highest total literacy rate of 69.54 percent, 80 : 30 percent in male literacy and 57.35 percent in female. On the other hand Belsand recorded the lowest rate of only 41.45 percent, 50.48 percent males and 30.89 percent of female literacy rate in 2001 census respectively. Similarly, sex ratio of small towns is also very revealing in North Bihar Plain. Mohiuddinnagar recorded 929 females/per 1000 males in the year 2001 and lowest sex ratio of 834 is found in Raghunathpur a newly emerged small towns in the region. Notwithstanding there, other attributes of socio-economic conditions resemble largely the 1991 pattern in the region.

The stagnation of small towns in growth perspective has tended to restrict the diversification of development processes. Urban policy therefore, must be oriented to creating network of knolls which will transform our traditional agriculture in to a modern commercial farming and create conditions for development of medium and small scale industries in smaller urban centres.

Small towns is closely connected with rural development. These towns have great economic opportunities which in turn, will absorb immigrants from rural areas and check the drain of emigrants destined to bigger cities of the state of elsewhere. During the course of population increment small towns of the previous decades have changed their size class. Further, the emerged administrative headquarters, viz C.D. Blocks and Sub-division headquarter market centers and role of transport services may emerged as new small towns. The role of small towns in district planning context is also notable because they may facilitate the action of development as points of connections between district Headquarters and large rural hinterlands. Under the circumstances, the role of small towns in overall economic structure of the region in rather limited. Even this limited role and its areal variations do not show any resemblance to special pattern of the economy. Small towns in the region have increased role to play in factoral development like agriculture, agro-based industries and building up of infrastructural components essential for economic reconstruction of North Bihar Plain.

Bibliography

Books :

Alber R. Adams, J.S. & Gould, p. 1971 Spatial Organisation, Prentice Hall, Inc., New Jersey.

Alexander, J.W. 1963 Economic Geography, Prentice Hall, Inc. New Jersey.

Ahmad, E. 1965 Bihar-Physical, Economic and Regional Geography, Ranchi University, Ranchi.

Ahmad, E & Singh, D.K. 1980 Regional Planning with Particular reference to India, Vol. II, Oriented Publishers & Distributors, New Delhi.

Ahmad, Q. 1965 Indian Cities- Characteristics and Correlates, University of Chicago, Chicago.

Akinchan, S. 1982 Urban Growth and Political Socialization in India, Janki Prakashan, Patna.

Ataullah, M. 1985 Urban Land-Its Use & Misuse, Amar Prakashan, Delhi

Barooah, G.L. 1985 Population Geography of Assam A Study in Dibrugarh Distt. 1872-1971, Mittal Publications, New Delhi.

Bagchi, K.G. & Pathan, C.R. 1974 Regional Development and Planning A Strategy, Calcutta.

Berry, B.J.L. & Marble, D.E. (Eds.) 1968 Spatial analysis, New Jersey.

Berry, B.J.L. & Harton, F.E. 1970 Geographic Perspective on Urban System, Prentice Hall, London.

Berry, B.J.L.& Kasarda, J.D. 1977 Contemporary Urban Ecology, Mc. Millon Publishing co., Inc., New York.

Berry, B.J.L. 1956 Goegraphical Aspects of the size and Arrangement of Urban Centres. M.A. Thesis, University of Washington.

Berry, B.J.L. & Garrison, W.L. 1957 A Probability model of the Distribution of city Sizes, Mimeographed manuscript, University of Washington.

Berry, B.J.L. & Pred, A. 1961 Central Place Studies : A Bibliography of theory and Application, Philadelphia.

Berry, B.J.L 1967 Geography Market Centres and Retail Distribution, Prentice Hall, Inc., Englewood Chiffs, New Jersey.

Bhargava, G. (ed.) 1981 Urban Problems and Policy in Perspective, Abhinav Publications, New Delhi.

Bhardwaj, R.K. 1974 Urban Development in India, National Publishing House, Delhi.

Bhattacharya, Bimlendu 1968 Functional Classification of Town in West Bengal, Paper for 21st International Geographical Congress held at New Delhi. Nov.-Dev., 1968, in S.P. Dasgupta and T.R. Lakshmanan (eds.) Abstracts of Papers, Calcutta, National Committee for Geography, pp. 270-71

Bogue, D.J. 1969 Principles of Demography, John wiley & Sons., Inc., New York.

Bonifatieva, L.I. 1971 Problems of Urban Planning in India, Economic and Socio Cultural Dimensions of Regionlisation, Census Continery Monograph, No. 7 New Delhi

Bose, Ashish 1966 Urbansiation in India : 1960-61, Studies in India's Urbanisation University Enclave, Delhi.

Bose, A 1959 The process of Urbanisation in India, 1901-51, University of Delhi (Unpublished Ph. D. Thesis)

Bose, A 1972 The Role of Small Towns in the Urabnisation process of India and Pakistan, Reading in Microlevel Planning and Rural Growth Centres (ed.) Lalit. K. Sen, NICD Hyderabad.

Bose, A. 1967 Patterns of Urban Growth in India, 1951-61 (ed.) Allied Publishers, New Delhi.

Bose, A. 1970 Urbanisation in India : An Inventory of Source Materials, Academic Book, Ltd., New Delhi.

Bose, A 1973 Studies in India's Urbanisation 1901-71, Tata Mc Graw Hill Publishing Company Ltd., New Delhi.

Breibanti & Spengler (ed.) 1961 Traditional Values and Socio-Economic Development, Derban.

Branch, M.C. 1975 Urban Planning Theory, Dowden Hachinson and Ross, Ince. Stroudsburg, Pensylvania.

Breese, G. 1969 Urbanisation in Newly Developing Countries, Prentice Hall of India, Pvt. Ltd., New Delhi.

Brouning, H.L. 1961 Method for Describing the Age-Sex Structure of Cities, in J.P. Gibbs (ed.), Urban Research Method Canada.

Brush, J.E. 1962 The Morphology of India Cities in Roy Turnor (ed.), India's Urban Feature, Selected Studies from an International Conference on Urbanisation in India, California.

Bryce, M.D. 1960 Industrial Development, Mc. Grow Hill Book Co., Inc., London.

Bulsara, J.F. 1964 Problems of Rapid Urbanisation in India, Bombay Popular Prakashan, Bombay.

Burgess, E.W. 1925 The growth of the City, in the City (ed.) Robert, E. Park, Earnest, W. Burgress and Roderick, D. Makenjee University of Chicago.

Carter, H. 1982 The Study of Urban Geography Edward Arnold, New Delhi

Chakrabarty, S.C. 1968 Population Density Gradients of Cities in S.P. Das Gupta and T.R. Laskhmanan (ed.) Abstract of Papers, Calcutta, National Committee for Geography, pp. 276-77.

Chandana, R.C. 1994 Introduction to population Geography, Kalyani Publishers, Ludhiana.

Chari, R.B. 1975 Demographic Trend in India, Essays Presented to Dr. Ashok Mitra, New Delhi, O.P. Sharma and R.K. Bhatia.

Chaplin, F.S. Jr. 1965 Urban Landuse Planning, The Unviersity of Illinois Press, illinois.

Cipolla, C.M. 1970 The Economic History of World Population, Penguin Books.

Choudhary, M.R. 1965 (ed.) Methodology in Urban Research-Eassay in Geography, (S.P. Chattarjee Volume), Calcutta, Geographical Society of India.

Choudhary, S.N. 1993 : "Geography of Floods in North Bihar, L.N.M.U. Press, Darbhanga.

Das, K.N. (ed.) 1967 Essays in Geography, Bhagalpur University, Bhagalpur.

Das, K.K.L. 1990 Population and Land Resource, Amit Prakashan, Patna.

Das Gupta, B. (ed.) 1988 Urbanisation, Migration and Rural Change,

A. Mukherjee & Co., Ltd. Calcutta.

Dayal, p. 1953 Bihar in Maps with Explanatory Text, Kusum Prakashan, Patna.

Dutta, B.B. 1977 Town Planning in Ancient India, New Asian Publishers, Delhi-6

Dutta, K.K. 1946 Introduction to Bihar' Patna.

Davis, Kingsley 1962 "Urbanisation in India-Past & Future" in Roy Turnor (ed.) India's Urban future selected study for an International conference on Urbanisation in India, Berkeley University of Californea Press.

Davis, Kingsley 1951 'The Population of India and Pakistan, Princeton University, Princeton.

Deshpande 1980 Impact of a Metropolitan City of Surrounding Regions, Concept Publishing Co., New Delhi.

Desai, P.B & Bose Ashish 1963 Planning and development of Sattelite and new Towns in Developing Countries-Economic Considerations" Delhi Institue of Economic Growth, Memeo)

Desai, P.B. et. al. (ed.) 1988 Regional perspective of Industrial and Urban Growth : The Case Study of Kanpur, Mcmillo9n & Co., Ltd. Calcutta.

Dickinson, R.E. 1947 City, Region & Regionalism, Oxford University Press, New York.

Dickinson, R.E. 1964 City and Region, A Geographical Interpretation, London,

Dickinson, R.E. 1972 City and Region, Routledge and Kajal Paul Ltd., London.

Dickinson, R.E. 1967 The Scope and Status of Urban Geography, Routledge and Kajal Paul Ltd. London.

Diwakar, R.R. 1959 Bihar Through the Ages, (ed.) Orient Longmans Pvt. Ltd., Calcutta.

Eversley, D. 1979 The Planner in Society, Feber, London.

Exline, C.H. Peters, G.L. & Larkin, R.P. 1982 The City; Pattern and Processes in Urban Ecosystem, West View Press inc., Colorado.

Freeman, T.W. 1958 Geography of planning, Hutchinson University Library, London.

Freedman, J. & Alonsow, w. 1967 Regional Development and Planning A Reader, M.I.T. Cambridge, Massachusetts.

Gallionm, A.B. & Eisher, S. 1965 The Urban Pattern, Affiliated East-West Press Pvt. Ltd., New Delhi.

Gernier, J.B & Chabot, G. 1967 Urban Geography, Longman's Grean & Co., London.

Garrison, W.L., 1959 Berry, B.J.F., Marble, D.F., Nystuan, J.D. & Morril, R.L. 1959 Studies of High way Development and Geographic Change, University of Washington Press, Seattle.

Geddes, Patrick 1952 Cities in Evolution, New & Revised Edition, New York, Oxford University Press.

Gibbs, J.B. 1966 Urban Research Methods, Affiliated East-West Press, Pvt. Ltd. New Delhi.

Gibbs, Jack B. 1961 Urban Research Method, D. Van Nostrand Co., Inc., Prinston, New Jersey.

Gilmore, H.W. 1953 Transportation and Growth of Cities, Glencoe, The Free Press Illinois.

Glikson, A. 1953 Regional Planning and Development, Hague.

Gosal, G.S. 1972 Urban Geography : A Trend Report 'Survey of Research in Geography'. Popular Prakashan, Bombay.

Gupta, G.R. 1983 "Urban India" Vikash Publishing House Pvt., Ltd., New Delhi.

Gupta, R.C. 1983 Growth Theory Strategy : A New Direction, Oxford University Press, New Delhi.

Green, F.H.W. 1961 "Urban Hinterlands in England and Wales : An analysis of Bus Service" in Jibbs, J.P. (ed.) Urban Research method, Canada.

Hagget, p. 1965 Location Analysis of Human Geography, Edward Arnold Ltd., London.

Hanser, P.M. 1956 World and Asian Urbanisation in Relation to **Size Classes of the town are as follows :**Economic Development and Social Change, New York.

Hanson, Niles, M. (1971) Intermediate Size Cities as Growth Centres : Application for Kentucky, The Piedmont Crescent, The Ozarks and Texas, Praeger Publication, Inc., New York.

Heer, D.M. 1969 Society and Poupulation Prantice Hall of India,

Pvt., Ltd., New Delhi.

Hilberseimer, L. 1955 The Nature of Cities, Chicago Paul Theobald and co. Chicago.

Hiresh, W.Z. 1973 Urban Economic Analysis, Mc Graw Hill Book Co., Inc., London.

Hudson, F.S. 1970 A Geography os Settlements, Macdonald and Evand Ltd., London.

Hudson, J.C. & Fowler, P.M. 1969 The Concept of Pattern in Geography, University of Lowa, Department of Geography.

Isard, W. 1960 Method of Regional Analysis: An Introduction to Regional Science, M.T.T. Press, London.

Isard, W. 1961 Method of Regional Analysis: Cambridge, Mass, M.T.T. press, London.

Jauhri, A.S. 1973 "Trend of Urbanisation in North West India in the Twentieth Century" In Urban Geography in developing countries by R.L. Singh. N.G.S.I. Varanasi.

Jha, B.N. 1980 Problems of Land Utilization, Classical Publications, New Delhi.

Jha, Bhogendra 1985 River Management of Flood Drought & Power Shortage in Bihar.

Jha, S.S. 1972 Political Elite in Bihar, Vora & Co., Bombay.

Jhonson, E.A.J. 1965 Market towns and Spatial Development in India, Nation Council of Applied Economic Research, New Delhi.

Jhonson, E.A.J. 1972 The Integration of Agrarian, Commercial and Industrial activities in Functional Economic Areas in NCAER, New Delhi.

Jones, E. 1966 Towns and Cities, Oxford Universtiy Press, London.

Karan, M.N. (ed.) 1981 Studies in Bihar's Economy and Society, Concept Publishing House, New Delhi.

Kashyap, S.S. 1975 Declining Sex-Ratioes in India, Demographic Trend in India (ed.) R.B. Chari.

King, L.J. 1969 Statistical Analysis in Goegraphy, Englewood Cliffs, Prentice Hall, New Jersey.

Keeple, L. 1964 Principle and Practices of Town and Country Planning, The Gazette Ltd., London.

Kulkarni, K.M. 1981 Urban Structure and Interaction: A Study of Nasik, City Region, Concept Publishing Company, New Delhi.

Kumar, A. 1985 Facets of Geomorphology, (ed.) Thinkers Library, Allahabad.

Lakshmanan, T.R. & S.P. Das Gupta (ed.) Geog 1968 "Siwan-A Sub-Regional Service Centres in Bihar", by R.S. Lal. National Committee for Geography, Calcutta.

Lewis, H.M. 1967 Planning the Modern City, John Willey & Sons. Inc., London.

Lewis, J.P. 1964 Quiet Crisis in India, Doubledej & Co. Inc., New York

Lipton, M. 1982 Why Poor People Stay Poor, Urban Dias in World Development Heritage Publishers, New Delhi.

Lokhathan, P.S. 1959 Techo-Econmic Survey of Bihar National Council of Applied Economic Research, New Delhi.

Losch, A. 1954 The Economic of Location, Translated by W.W. Waglom, Bostal.

Mandal, R.B. & (ed.) Sinha, U.N.P. 1980 Recent Trends and Concepts in Geograpjy, Vol. III, Comcept Publishing co., New Delhi.

Mandal, R.B. 1981 Planned Development of Rural Settlement, Concept Publishing Co., New Delhi.

Mandal, R.B. & Peters, G.L. (ed.) 1982 Urbanisation and Regional Development, Concept Publishing Co., New Delhi.

Mayor, H.M. & Kohn, C.F. 1967 Reading in Urban Geography, Central Book Depot, Allahabad.

Minocha, A.C. & Yadav, H.S. 1989 Small & Medium Towns & Their Role in Regional Development. Special Reference to Madhya (Pradesh) Gyan Publishing House New Delhi.

Mitra, et. al. 1980 An ICSSR a JNU Study on "Population and Area of Cities Towns and Urban Agglomerations, (1872-1971), Allied Publishers Pvt. Ltd., New Delhi.

Mishra, R.P. Mahadev, P.D. & Jayshankar, D.C. 1972 Urban System and Regional Development (Part one). Prasaranga University, Mysore.

Mishra, R.P. Sundaram, K.V. & Natraj, V.K. 1978 (ed.) Regional Planniong and National Development, Vikash Publishing House, Pvt. Ltd., Delhi-6

Mishra, D.K. 1994 ,Vandinin Mahananda, In Hindia Sanata Prakashan Pvt. Ltd., Patna.

Mishra, K.K. 1953 Aithihasic Mahatua-Mithila Ka Itihas (in Hindi), Mithila Prakashan, Laheriasarai, Darbhanga.

Mitra, Ashok 1967 "A Functional Classification of India's Towns" In Ashish Bose (ed.), Patterns of Population Change in India, Allied Publishers, New Delhi.

Moore, W.E. 1969 The Impact of Industry, Prentice Hall of India, Pvt. Ltd., Delhi.

Mukherjee, R.K. 1968 Man and its Habitation, Popular Prakashan, Bombay.

Murphy, R.E. 1966 The American City : An Urban Geography, Mc Grow Hill Book Co. New York.

Nagia, S. 1976 Delhi Metropolitan Region : A Case Study of Settlement Geography K.B. Publications, New Delhi.]

Noble, Allen, G. & Ashok K. Dutta 1977 (Ed.) Indian Urbanization and Planning, Vehicles of Modernization, Tata Mc Grow Hill Publishing Co. Ltd., Delhi-2

Orbans, P. & Orbans, M. 1976 Urban Life : Diversity and Inequality, W.M.C. Brown Co., Babque, Jawa.

O' Riordan, T. 1971 Perspectives on Resource Management, Pion, London.

Pal, S.K. 1968 Urban Trends of Metropolitan Cities of India, in S.P. Das Gupta and T.R. Lakshmanan (Ed.) National Committee of Geography, Calcutta.

Pandey, P. 1970 Impct of Urbanization of Urban Growth : A Case Study of Chotanagpur, Central Book Depot, Allahabad.

Rao, R.R.M. 1981 Growth of Cities : A Case study of Warangal, Studies Publications, New Delhi.

Rao, V.L.S.P. 1966 Regional Pianning, Asia Publishing House, Delhi.

Ratcliffe, J. 1981 An Introduction to Town and Country Planning, Hutchinson & Co., Ltd., London.

Robson, B.T. 1973 Urban Growth : An Approach, Mathuen & Co. Ltd., London.

Richard, J.C. & Hugget, P. 1967 Models in Geography, Mathuen & Co. London.

Robert, M. 1974 An Introduction to Town Planning Techniques, Hutchinson & Co. Ltd., London.

Rothermad, D. et. al. (ed.) 1980 Urban Growth and Rural Stagnation, Studies in t he Economy of an Indian Coalfield and its rural Hinterland, Manohar Publications, New Delhi.

Singh, J. 1964 Transport Geography of South Bihar, B.H.U. Press, Varanasi,

Singh, R.P. 1969 Geomorphological Evolution of Chotanagpur Highland -India, N.G.S.I. Varanasi.

Singh, R.P. & Kumar, Anil 1970 Monograph of Bihar Bharati Bhawan, Patna.

Singh, R.L. & Rana, P.B. (ed.) 1979 Place of Small Towns in India, N.G.S.I., Varanasi.

Singh, O.P. 1979 Nagariya Bhoogol, Tara Publication, Varanasi (Hindi)

Singh, U. 1961 Allahabad : A Study in Urban Geography, N.G.S.I. Varanasi

Singh, V.N. 1986 Spatial Urban Pattern and Growth of Urbanization, Inter India Publications New Delhi.

Singh, G.N. & Singh, D.P. 1987 Some Aspects of Population Studies in India, Sadhana Mudranalya, Munger.

Smailes, A.E. 1953 The Geography of Towns, Hutchinson University Library, London.

Solesbury, 1974 Policy in Urban Planning, Perganmon, London.

Stallery & Mores 1965 Modern Small Industry for Developing Countries, Mc Grow Hill Book Co. Delhi.

Stamp, L.D. 1960 Applied Geography, Penguine Books, London.

Tailor, T.G. 1951 Urban Geography, Methuen & Co., London.

Thimmiah, G. 1985 Burning Issue in Centre State Financial Relation, Ashish Publishing House, New Delhi.

Tripathi, Havaldar (Sohridai) 1977 Bihar Ki Nadiyan, Hindi Granth Academy, Bihar, Patna.

Trivedi, H.R. 1975 Urbanization & Micro-Social Change, Chugh Publications, Allahabad.

Uzzell, J.D. & provencher, R. 1976 Urban Anthropology, W.M.C. Brown Co. Publishers, Dubuque, Lowa.

Wadhera, K. 1983 Urban Fringe Land Markets, Concept Publishing Co., New Delhi.

Wishwakarma, R.K. 1981 Urban & Regional Planning Policy in India, Uppal Publisihng House, New Delhi.

Wishwakarma, R.K. & Jha, G. (Ed.) 1983 Integrated Development of Small & Medium Towns : Problems and Strategic Policy Issue, Times Press, New Delhi.

B. Thesis :

Agues, M. 1969 Manglore : A Study in Uraban Geography, Ph. D. Thesis, Patna.

Jha, S.N. 1989 Small Towns of Bihar : A Study in Urban Regional Planning Strategy, Ph. D. Thesis, L.N.M.U. Darbhanga.

Jha, T. 1984 North Bihar : A Study in Regional Planning, Ph.D. Thesis L.N.M.U. Darbhanga.

Jha, K.D. 1993 Urban Agglomeration of Bihar : A Study in Problems of Concentration and Urban Settlement Planning, Ph.D. Thesis, L.N.M.U. Darbhanga.

Chandra, K.S. 1967 Pressure of Population of Land of Bihar, Ph.D. Thesis, Bhagalpur University.

Chakravarty P. 1986 Integrated Development of Darbhanga City Urbanised Zone : An Approach to Micro-Reginal Planning, Ph.D. Thesis, L.N.M.U. Darbhanga.

Karimi, S.M. 1967 : Urban Settlement in Bihar Plain Ph.D. Thesis, Aligarh Muslim University.

Khan, M.S. 1970 Planning for Urban-Industrial Growth of Chotanagpur, M.R.P. Thesis, I.I.T., Kharagpur.

Mukherjee, M. 1966 Functions and Functional Classifications of Towns in Bihar, Ph. D. Thesis, Patna University.

Thakur, B. 1983 Rural-Urban Fringe of Darbhanga, Ph. D. Thesis, Bihar University, Muzaffarpur.

Papers, Journals and Periodicals :

Annals of American Association of Geographers :

Webb, J.N. 1959 Basic Concepts in the Analysis of Small Urban Centres of Minesota, Vol. XLIX, No. 1-4, 1959.

Economic Geography

Karan, P.P. 1953 Economic Regions of Chotanagpur, Bihar, India, Vol. 29.

Ekistics

Hughes, J.T. & Hoslowski, J. 1969 Threshold Analysis on Economic tool for Towns and Country Planning, Vol. 27, No. 161.

Lal, A. & Tirtha, R. 1969 India's Urbanisation, Vol. 27, No. 161

Lasuen, J.R. 1970 On Growth Poles, Vol. 30 No. 180

Papaioannou, J.G. 1970 Future Urbanisation Patterns : A Long Henge World Wide View, Vol. 20 No. 173.

Geographical Knowledge

Mukherjee, M. 1970 Trade Towns of Bihar vol. 3.

Geographical Outlook

Karimi, S.M.1969 Zones of Urban Concentration in Bihar, Vol. VI.

Pandey, p. 1976 Some Aspects of Quantification in Geography, Vol. XI.

Prasad, M. & Oraon, A. 1976 Rank Correlation Methods : Application to the Problem of Spatial Grouping, Vol. XI.

Verma, L.N. 1975 Spatial Hierarchy of Urban Settlemtns, vol. X.

Singh, D.K. & Singh, K.K. 1978 Central Functions and Centrality of Settlements in Palamu District, Vol. VIII.

Siddique, M. 1978 An Approach to Comparative Urban Geography, Vol. VIII.

Sahu, S.K. 1979 Trend of Urbanisation in Upper Mahanadi Basin in Orissa, Vol. XIV.

Jafri, S.S.A. 1980 Industrial Classification and Hierarchical Orders ot Towns in the North Eastern Region of India (1971) Vol. XV.

Singhal, G.d. 1983 Geographical Appraisal of the Integrated Urban Development of Magadh Plain, Bihar, Vol. XVII.

Geographical Review of India

Basu, T.K. 1975 Functional Classification of Urban Settlements in Singhbhum District, Bihar, Cartographical Appraisal, Vol. 38.

Karennavar, M.F. 1976 A Quantitative Analysis of the Pattern of Urban Settlements in Karnataka State, Vol. 38.

Kumar, A. & Sharma, N. 1974 Spatial Arrangement and Degree of Specialisation of Urban Centres, Vol. 36.

Mukherjee, A.B. 1973 Levels of Urbanisation in U.P. Vol. XXV.

Munsi, S.K. 1973 An Enquiry into Urban Stagnation in the small Towns in West Bengal, Vol. XXXV.

Munsi, S.K. 1975 The Nature of Indian Urbanisation : A Review, Vol. 37.

Pathak, C.R. 1973 Integrated Area Development, Vol. XXXV.

Sen, p. 1974 Application of Q-Technique to Identify a Growth Centre, Vol. 36.

Sharma, P.R. 1975 Growth Pole Strategy in Regional Planning in Identifiaction and Interpretation, Vol. XXXVII.

Thakur, B. 1976 Spearman Rank Correleation Coefficient : A Review of Technique and Applications in Geographical Research. vol. XXXVIII.

Dutta. B. 1983 Economic Planning and Regional Imbalance, Vol. XXXXV, No.1.

Roy, p. 1983 Spatio-Temporal Aspects of City Size Distributions in India, 1901-81, Vol. XXXXV, No. 1.

Lahiri, S. 1984 Levels of Urbanisation in Burdwan District in 1981 : A Quantitavie Analysis, vol. XXXXVI, No. 2.

Indian Journal of Regional Science

Elhance, A 1984 Soceial Overhead Capital and Regional Development : An Analytial Framwork, Vol. XVI, No. 1.

Rontray, S.K. 1984 Approaches to Backward District Planning : Case of Boudh-Khoudhmals District in Orissa, Vol. XVI, No. 1

Deka, P. 1986 Spatial and Temporal Urbanisation in N.E. India- 1961-81. Vol. XVIII, No. 1.

Mehta, B.C. 1986 Choice of Appropriate Scale and Sectors in Industrialisation in a Backward Region, Vol.XVIIIl No. 1.

Indian Geographical Studies

Mandal, R.B. 1974 Rank Size Relationship of Towns in Bihar Plain, No. 3.

Mandal, R.B. 1976 Urban Potential in Bihar, No. 6.

Sinha, V.N.P. 1974 Hierarchy of Trade Towns in Bihar, No. 3.

Thakur, B. 1973 Nearest Neighbour Analysis as a Measure of Urban Place Patterns, No.1.

Singh, R.P. 1980 Growth of Small Scale Industry and Its Impact on the Economy of the Bihar Plain, Bulletin, No. 14.

Prasad, B. 1981 Role of Master Plan in Urban Development, Bulletin No. 16.

Verma, R.S.P. 1983 Role of Small Industries in Urban Development, Bulletin, No. 21.

National Geographical Journal of India :

Mukherjee, M. 1970 Aspects of Recent Industrialisation in Chotanagpur, Vol. XVI, pt. 2.

Reddy, N.B.K. 1970 Urban Evolution Growth Pattern and Urbanisation Trends in the Krishna & Godawari Deltas, vol XIV.

Mishra, S.K. 1980 Modification of Growth Centres Strategy for Rural Development in Under Developed countries, Vol. XVI Part 3 &4.

Singh, A.N. 1982 Trend of Urbanisation in Malwa (M.P.) Vol. XXVIII, Part 3 & 4.

Singh, M.K. & Singh, B.N. 1983 Urban Trend and Urban Landuse Pattern in South Mirzapur, U.P. Vol XXIX, Part 1 & 2.

Bala, R. 1984 Urbanisation in Rajasthan State : 1981, Vol. XXX, Part I.

Singh, K.N., Singh, S.B. & singh, B.B. 1985 Service Centres and Development Strategy in Vindhyachal-Beghel-Khand Region : A Spatio-Functional Approach, Vol. XXXI, Part 2.

Singh, R.L. 1985 Ecology of UrbanHabitat and Environmental Planning in India, Vol. XXI, Part 4.

Roy, B.K. 1986 Recent Urbanisation in India : A Scenario, Vol. XXXII, Part I.

National Geographer

Maurya, S.d. & Devi, G. 1984 Trends of Urbanisation in Uttar Pradesh, Vol. 19, No. 1.

Singh, K.N. 1984 Transportation Network and Level of Urbansiation : A Case Study of Eastern U.P., Vol. 19, No.1.

The Deccan Geographer

Jain, N.G. & Layer, L. 1980 Urban Spatial Pattern in Maharashtta, Vol. XVIII, No.1.

Singh, R.N. 1982 Occupational Structure of Urban Centres of Eastern Uttar Pradesh-A Case Study of Manufacturing, Vol. XX, No.1.

Khatu, K.K. 1982 Urban Land Use Strategy in Welfare State, Vol, XX, No. 2.

Diddee, J. & Datye, V.S. Use of Settlement Hierarchy in Identification of growth Centres for regional Planning Poona District, Vol. XX & XXI, Nos. 3 & 1

Seetharaman, S. 1985 An Approach to the Understanding of the Occupational structure of Small Towns in Tanjore District in Tamilnadu, Vol. XXIII, No. 1.

The Geographer :

Sundaram, K.V. 1981 Techniques and Methods of Resource Based Regionalisation in Inida, Vo. XXVIII, No. 1.

Aziz, A. 1982 Orthogenesis of Towns of Uttar Pradesh, vol. XXIX, No. 1.

Aziz, A. 1983 Man-Land Ratio in the Towns of Uttar Pradesh, Vol XXX, No. 2.

The Indian Geographical Journal

Vasantha, (Mrs.) V. 1981 Growth and Development of Towns in Tamilnadu, 1901-1981, Vol. LVI, No. 2.

Chakraverty, S.C. 1982 Regional Planning : A Framwork of Operation, Vol. LVII, No. 1.

Desai, A.P. 1983 Place— Prosparity Versus People Prosperity : A Vital Issue in Regional Planning, Vol. LVIII No. 10

Mehta (Mrs.) S. & Sharma, S. 1985 Locational Conflicts in Small Twons : A Case Study of a Co-operative Sugar Mill in Punjab, Vol. LX, No. 1.

Town Planning Review

Herbert, D.T. & Rane, J.W. 1976 Defining Communities within Urban Areas : An Analysis of Alternative Approaches, Vol. 47, No. 4.

Travis, A.S. 1977 Planning as Applied Ecology : The Management of Alternative Future, Vol. 48, No.1.

Bristow, M.R. 1978 Regional Planning : A Review Articles, Vol. 49,

No. 1.

Khox, L.P. 1978 Territorial Social Indicators and Area Profiles : Some Cautionary Observations, Vol. 49. No. 1.

Baxter, R.S. & Rane, J.W. 1979 Forecasting Financial Resources in Regional Planning, vol. 50.

Madden, M. 1979 Recent Development in Urban Dynamics : Review Article, Vol. 50, No. 2.

Uttar Bharat Bhoogol Patrika

Chand, R.P. 1984 Changes in Centrality and Urban Hierarchy in Awadh Region, Vol. Xx, No. 2...

Verma, S.S. 1985 Level of Urbanisation in Rohilkhand (U.P.) Vol. XXI, No. 2.

Reprints :

Kumar, A. & Sharma, N. 1973 Correlation of Spatial Arrangements and Specialisation of Urban Centres in Chotanagpur, Uttar Bharat Bhoogol Patrika, Vol. IX, No. 3.

Sharma, N. 1972 Degree of Urbanisation and Level of Economic Development in Chotanagpur 'ISRS' Vol. IV, No. 2. Kharagpur.

Sharma, N. 1975 On Some Aspects of Urbanisation in Bihar India, Bhagalpur University Journal, Vol. VIII, No. 3 (Social Science), Bhagalpur.

Sharma, N. 1977 Theory of Regional Development : A Study in Resource ?Endowment & Regional Economic Growth, Journal of the Bhagalpur University, Social Science Vol. X, No.3. Bhagalpur.

Sharma, N. 1978 Measurement of Unevenness in Distribution of Urban Population in Bihar : An Approach to Regionalisation, 'The North Eastern Geographer,' Vol. X. No. 1 & 2.

Sharma, N. 1980 Temporal Dimensions of Urban Geography, 'Recent Trends and Concepts in Geography' (ed.) R.B. Mandal & V.N.P. Sinha, Concept Publishing Co., New Delhi.

Sharma, N. 1982 Town Oriented Resource Based Urban Regional Planning : A Planning Strategy Applied to the State of Bihar (India), Urbanisation and Regional Development', (ed) R.B. Mandal & G.L. Peters, concept Publishing Co., New Delhi.

Others :

Sharma, N. & Jha, S.N. 1985 Spatio-Temporal Study of Pace of Urbanisation, In Bihar, 'Bihar : A Physical Economic and Regional Geography & Planning (ed.) P. Dayal et. al., Janki Prakashan, Patna (Unpublished).

Sharma, N. & Mishra, K.K. 1985 Spatio Temporal study of Scale of Urbanisation in Bihar 'Ibid'

Singh, R.P. 1961 Topography and Town in the Chotanagpur Highlands, Prac. 48th. Indian Science Congress.

India Habitate-76, The U.N. Conference on Human Settlements, Vancouver, 1976.

Proceedings : International Conference of Urban & Regional Change in Developing Countries, I.I.T., Kharagpur, Dec. 12-14, 1981

Reports and Government Publications :

Bihar : District Census Hand Books, 1981 (Series-4).

Bihar : Provisional Population Tables-1981 (Series-4), Pert IIA

Bihar : General Population Tables-1981 (Series-4), Part II.

Bihar : General Economic Tables, (Series-4), Part III A & B.

Bihar : Town Directory (Series-4), Part X-A

Bihar : Census Atlas, (Series-4) Part IX, 1961 & 1971

Bihar : General Report on Census-1961, Series-4, Part I (A).

Bihar : Through Figures, 1981, 82, 83, & 84 Directorate of Statistics and Evalution, Govt. of Bihar.

Selected Plan Statistics-1984, Directorate of Statistics Evaluation, Govt. of Bihar.

Draft Perspective Plan (1979-89), Bihar State Planning Board, Govt. of Bihar, Patna.

Mineral Statistics of India- 1983.

Electricity Board at a Glance, 1984-85, Bihar State Electricity Board, Patna.

Draft Sixth Five Year Plan, Planning Commission, Govt. of India (1980-85), New Delhi.

Report of the Task Force on "Planning and Development of Small and Medium Towns as Cities" Govt. of India, Ministry of Works and Housing-1977.

Census of India, 1961- An Approach to Urban Studies in India (ed.) B.K. Roy, Burman, 1971.

Report of Committee on Urban Works, Pt. I, Govt. of India, Ministry of Works and Housing. New Delhi. 1976.Draft Master Plan: Maner, Rajgir, Bodh Gaya, Netarhat, Koilwar.

Census of India, 2001, Provisional Population Totals, Series 4, Bihar.

APPENDIX-I

Small Towns of North Bihar Plain : Area and Pouplation, 1991

Sl. No.	Small Towns	District in Which located	Towns Status	Area in km²	Popul ation	Persons Per Km²
1.	Mirganj	Gopalganj	N.A.A.	5.48	19697	3594.34
2.	Chanpatia	Paschim Champaran	N.A.C.	7.57	19320	2552.17
3.	Katihar Rly. Colony	Katihar	N.A.C.	N.A.	18931	N.A.
4.	Motipur	Muzaffarpur	N.A.C.	12.77	17821	1395.53
5.	Manihari	Katihar	N.A.C.	11.31	17252	1525.37
6.	Maharajganj	Siwan	N.A.C.	7.60	17165	2258.55
7.	Jainagar	Madhubani	N.A.C.	1.55	16978	10953.54
8.	Chchatapur	Saharsa	N.A.C.	3.69	16746	4538.21
9.	Dalsingsarai	Samastipur	N.A.C.	2.94	16738	5693.19
10.	Kanti	Muzaffarpur	N.A.C.	16.16	16037	992.38
11.	Mairwa	Siwan	N.A.C.	6.23	15215	2442.21
12.	Birpur	Saharsa	N.A.C.	8.67	14742	1700.34
13.	Belsand	Sitamarhi	N.A.C.	10.09	14151	1402.47
14.	Sheohar	Sitamarhi	N.A.C.	9.33	13915	1491.42
15.	Nirmali	Saharsa	N.A.C.	5.30	13783	2600.56
16.	Chakia	Purbi Champaran	N.A.C.	6.23	13708	2200.32
17.	Thakurganj	Kishanganj	N.A.C.	10.46	13589	1299.13
18.	Katiya	Gopalganj	N.A.C.	11.13	13336	1198.20
19.	Barauni I.O.C.	Begusarai	N.A.C.	2.53	12594	4977.86
20.	Ghoghardiha	Madhubani	N.A.C.	8.73	12020	1376.86
21.	Dumra	Sitamarahi	N.A.C.	2.28	11632	5101.75
22.	Samastipur Rly. Colony	Samastipur	N.A.C.	N.A.	11589	N.A.
23.	Mohiuddinagar	Smastipur	N.A.C.	8.08	11012	1362.87
24.	Rajopatti Talkhapur	Sitamarhi	N.A.C.	3.42	10769	3148.83
25.	Janakpur Road (Pupari)	Sitamarhi	N.A.C.	3.10	9590	3093.54
26.	Lauthaha	Purbi Champaran	N.A.C.	1.59	5823	3662.26
27.	Bhimnagar	Saharsa	N.A.C.	8.86	5673	640.29
	North Bihar Plain			175.1	379826	2169-km²

Source : Census of India, 1991 : Townwise P.C.A., NIC Unit, Patna.

APPENDIX-II

Small Towns of North Bihar Plain : Area and Pouplation, 1991

Sl. No.	Small Towns	District in Which located	Towns Status	Area in km²	Popul ation	Persons Per Km²
1.	Sugauli	Paschim Champaran	N.A.C.	19.25	19644	1020
2.	Lalganj	Vaishali	M	7..6	19535	2485
3.	Bihariganj	Saharsa	N.A.C.	17.75	19049	1073
4.	Gogri Jamalpur	Munger	N.A.C.	9.49	18896	1991
5.	Rosera	Samastipur	M	1.08	18599	18057
6.	Jogbani	Purnia	N.A.C.	15.12	18461	1221
7.	Banmanki Bazar	Purnia	N.A.C.	20.15	17491	668
8.	Mirganj	Gopalganj	N.A.C.	5.48	17337	3164
9.	Dighwara	Saran	N.A.C.	13.27	17072	12.87
10.	Murliganj	Saharsa	N.A.C.	14.07	16804	1194
11.	Bahadurganj	Purnia	N.A.C.	29.17	16786	575
12.	Chanpatia	Paschim Champaran	N.A.C.	7.57	16083	2050
13.	Jhanjharpur	Madhubani	N.A.C.	12.44	15303	1230
14.	Maharajganj	Siwan	N.A.C.	7.60	15196	1999
15.	Dalsingsarai	Samastipur	N.A.C.	2.94	13413	4562
16.	Birpur	Saharsa	N.A.C.	8.67	12953	1494
17.	Manihari	Katihar	N.A.C.	11.34	12592	1113
18.	Jainagar	Madhubani	N.A.C.	1.55	11955	7713
19.	Mairwa	Siwan	N.A.C.	6.23	11946	1917
20.	Belsand	Sitamarahi	N.A.C.	10.09	10804	1071
21.	Thakurganj	Purnia	N.A.C.	10.46	10760	1029
22.	Nirmali	Saharsa	N.A.C.	5.34	10108	1907
23.	Chakia	Purbi Champaran	N.A.C.	6.23	9608	1542
24.	Mohiuddinagar	Samastipur	N.A.C.	8.08	8805	1090
25.	Janakpur road (Pupri)	Sitamarhi	N.A.C.	3.10	6493	2240
	North Bihar Plain			254.29	366143	1440/km²

Source : Census of India, 1981, Series-4 : Bihar, Town Directory of Bihar, Patna.

Appendix-III

Measurement of Serviceability and Efficiency of Small Towns : Criteria For Scoring :

Variables/Categories			Assigned Score
1. Civic/Administrative Status:			
i.	a.	District H.Q.	3
	b.	Sub-Division H.Q.	2
	c.	Block H.Q.	1
ii.	a.	Corporation City	4
	b.	Municipality/Cantonment	3
	c.	Notified Area Committe	2
	d.	Census Town	1
2. Road Facilities:			
i.	Lengthe of Rd Per km^2		
	a.	above 5 km.	4
	b.	2.5-5km.	3
	c.	1.0-2.5 km	2
	d.	Less than 1.00 km.	1
ii	Pressure of Population on Rd Per Kms:		
	a.	Below 1000 Population	3
	b.	1000-5000 population	2
	c.	More than 5000 population	
3. Railway Facilities :			
i.	Pressure per train :		
	a.	Below 1000	4
	b.	1000-3000	3
	c.	3000-5000	2
	d.	Above 5000	1
4. Severge :			
	a.	Pucca	3
	b.	Mixed	2
	c.	Kachcha	1
5. Disposal of Night Soil :			
	a.	Tractor	3
	b.	Trolly	2
	c.	Private/Head	1
6. Water Supply/Load in Gallons:			
	a.	Above 20 thousand	4

	b.	10-20 thousand	3
	c.	1-10 thousand	2
	d.	Below 10 thousand	1

7. Electrification :

1.		Domestic (No. of house electrified)	
	a.	Above 95%	3
	b.	80-95%	2
	c.	Less than 80%	1
ii		Industrial (Units Consuming Electricity)	
	a.	above 50%	4
	b.	25-50%	3
	c.	1-25%	2
	d.	Less than 1%	1
iii		Commercial (Units Consuming Electricity) :	
	a.	above 75%	4
	b.	50-75%	3
	c.	25-50%	2
	d.	Less than 25%	1
iv.		Road lightening Points Per km. Road :	
	a.	above 100	5
	b	50-100	4
	c.	25-50	3
	d.	10-25	2
	e.	Less than 10	1

8. Commodities exported :

a.	Primary Agricultural Products (Food Grains)	1
b.	Cash Crops/Rail Material	2
c.	Processed	3

9. Commodities Exported :

a.	Cash crop/raw Material	3
b.	Processed	2
c.	Preserved Food grains	1

10. Commodities Manufactured at :

a.	Cottage/Small Scale	1
b.	Heavy/Medium	2
c.	High-Technology	3

11. Financial Centre :

i. Banks/Served Area in Km^2:

a. Less than 0.1 Km^2 3
b. 0.1-0.5 Km^2 2
c. Above 0.5 km^2 1

ii. Pressure of Population Per Banks:
a. Above 5000 persons 1
b. 1000-5000 persons 2
c. 500-1000 persons 3
d. Less than 500 persons 4

12. Educational Facilities :

i. No. of Unit/km^2 :
a. above 10 4
b. 5-10 3
c. 1-5 1
d. Less than 1 1

ii Population Pressure per Unit :
a. Less than 1000 4
b. 1000-5000
c. 5000-10000 2
d. Above 10000 1

13. Health Service:

i. Average Served area per unit :
a. Above 10 km^2 1
b. 5-10 km^2 2
c. 1-5 km^2 3
d. Less than 1 km^2 4

ii. Pressure of Population per Unit :
(of available health facilities)
a. Less than 100 4
b. 1000-5000 3
c. 5000-10000 2
d. Above 10000 1

14. Recreational/Cultural Facilities :

i. No. of Facilities per km^2
a. above 10 per km^2 4
b. 5-10 per km^2 3
c. 1-5 per km^2 2
d. Less than 1 per km^2 1

ii Existing Pressure of Population Per unit :

a. Less than 500 4
b. 500-1000 3
c. 1000-5000 2
d. Above 5000 1

15. Communicational Links :

a. River-Airways 1
b. Bus Roadways 2
c. Railway 3

16. Nearest City :

a. Within 10 km. Periphery 3
b. 10-50 km. Periphery 2
c. Out of 50 Km. 1

Appendix-IV

Statement V
CIVIC & OTHER AMENITIES IN TOWNS 1991

Sl. Name of Towns	Towns Status	1991 Population	S/C S/T Population	Road Length in kms	System of sewerage	Number of Laterines: water booms	Number of Laterines: servioe	Number of Laterines: others	Method disposal soil	Protected supply source ice	Water capacity	Fire fighting serv	Electrification (number of connections): domestic	industrial	commercial	road lighthing	rail up	Down
1. JanakpurRd.	N.A.C. 1631	9590 Km	S/C Nala S/T 31	3.10² K.Rd-3 km P-Rd-1 km.	Pucca Nala	Septic	"	x	Head	OST 15000 gal.	T.W+W Road tube	Sitam-arhi 27km.	80%	3	13	x	3	3
2. Thakurganj	N.A.C	13589	S/C 801 S/T 607	10.46 km² Kr-5.1 Km. P.R.-10 Km²	Kuccha Nala	Septic	AFew	Sulabh	Trolly	WT OST 250,000	T.W. Road Tape	Kishan-ganj 50	75%	2%	23%	53	3	3
3. Birpur	NAC	14742	S/C 920 ST-21	5/8 km² pp. 2550	Pucca	Septic	x	"	x	OST 250000	T.W. W.I.	Saharsa	06%	x	x	4	-	-
4. Murliganj	NAC	17165	SC-1124 ST-141	4.04 Km.	Kacha	Septic	x	-	Trolly	-	T.W.,	Siwan	75%	x	25%	-	0	0
5. Chakia	NAC	13708	SC-1956 ST-10	6 km.	Pucca Kaccha Nala	Septic	-	Sulabh	Private	-	T.W/W	Motih-ari	75%	20%	5%	-	3	3
6. Jainagar	NAC	16978	SC-3186 ST-25	2,1/2, kms	Half Pucca Kaccha	Septic	A few	-	Head	OST/WT 150000	T.W/W	Madh-ubani 26km	80%	20%	5%	-	3	3
7. Dalsingsarai	NAC	16738	SC-2026 ST-036	2.94	Half Pucca Kaccha	Spetic	A few	-	Trolly	Os-WT 10,000	TW/W	Samas tipur 26 km.	75%	25%	-	-	3	3
8. Ghoghardiha	NAC	12020	SC-1740 ST-35	1.73	Kaccha Nala	Service Spetic	A few	-	Head	-	TW/W	Madhubani 60km.		85%	5%	10	3	3

Town Directory | Statement V | Appendix-IV (ii)

MEDICAL, EDUCATIONAL, RECREATIONAL AND CULTURAL FACILITIES IN TOWNS-1991

Sl. Name of	Population	Medical Facilities		Educational Facilities											Recreational and Cultural Facilities			
Towns	1991	Hospital Dispenary Trg. Cen.	Beds Hospital Col.	Arts, Sc., Com.	Medical College.	Engi. College	Poly. tech.	Short. hand- Voca-	High Seh-. ool	Sec Sch.	Middle ool.	Prim. Sh. ool.	Adu. Edu.	Womens Hostel	Station	Line-	Ace. di	Pub- Libraries
1. Janakpur Rd	9590	Pri. Health	5	x	UBG 43 km.	MIT. Muz. 60 km	DBG 4 km	3	21	2	2	2	-	-	-	-	1club	x
2. Thakurganj	13589	Dispen.1	x	1	KSG. 80 km	Bhag-alpur	Purnia 125km	2	2	M/F	M-2 F-1	5	x	x	x	2	x	x
3. Birpur	17000	Sadar Hos. T.B. Ward	10	1	DBG. 140km	Muz. 200km.	Saharsa 110 km.	3	1	1	3	2	x	x	x	2 -	x	1
4. Maharajganj	17165	Hos. & Heal, Cen-6	6	3	MUZ. 120km	MUZ. 200km	ITI Siwan	3	3	1	4	6	x	x	x	2 -	x	1
5. Chakia	13708	Sadar Hos.	-	1	MUZ. 48km.	MUZ. 48km.	-	-	-	2	2	5	-	x	1	3 -	1	1
6. Jainagar	16978	Hos. & Heal. Cen.	6	3	DBG. 68km.	M.I.T. MUZ.	No	2	2	-	3	1	x	-	2	--	-	1
7. Dalsingsarai	16738	Hos. & Health Cent.	6	2	-	-	No	3	3	3	2	4	-	x	-	2	-	2
8. Ghoghardiha	12020	Health Cent.	2	2	DEG. 63km.	MI.T MUZ.	DBG. 63km.	1	-	1	2	3	-	x	-	1	-	1

Statement VI
TRADE COMMERCE AND BANKING

Sl.	Name of Towns	Number of Three Most important commodities Imported			Number of Three Most important commodities Imported			Number of Three Most important commodities Manufact			Numbr of Bakns	Number of Agri.socie-ties.	Number of Non-Agri. Credit Soc.	Others any
1.	Janakpur Road	Rice	Wheat	Oil	Seed Oil	SeedRice	Pulse	-	-	-	4	2	2	Block Hd. Qr. -
2.	Thakurganj	Rice	Dalda	Potato	Jute	Chillies	Tea & Tejpatta	Rice Mill	Eng. Greel Iron.	Wood ply	2	1	1	Block Hd.Qr. Sub-div. Proposed
3.	Birpur	Rice	Wheat	Potato	Jute	Cercal		Rice	Power	Wood ply	4	1	1	Sub.div HQ. Raghopur 35km
4.	Maharajganj	Rice	Wheat	Potato	Gud	Patsan	Pulse	Gud	Chura	Pulse/ Jute Mill	3	2	5	S.D.O. Siwan D.C.L.R. 20 km Block HQ./ NAC PHED.
5.	Chakia	Rice	Wheat	Maize	Khadhi	Sugar	M.Oil	Sugar	M.Oil	Dal mill	3	1	1	S.D.O. Cold Storage.
6.	Jainagar	Rice	Wheat	Oil Seed	M.Oil	Rice Product	Wheat	M.Oil	Steel Product	Repair	3	2	3	S.D.O./ Block HQ. Distt. MBI. 36 km
7.	Dalsinghsarai	Rice	Wheat	Tobacco	M.Oil	Rice Product	Chilli	Wood	Steedl Product	Repair	3	1	2	S.D.O/ Block HQ. Dist. Samastipur 20kms
8.	Ghogardiha	Rice	Wheat	Pulse	M.Oil	Rice Product	Sugar cane	Steel Product	Rice	Maize	2	1	2	Block HQ. Madhubani 46km

Source : Data Collected From Notified Area Committee Office Personally in the Sample Towns during October-November, 1996.

North Bihar Plain : Service Scores of Small Towns
Scores
124 Variables

Sl. No.	Small Towns																									Total Scores
1.	Janakpur road	1	2	3x5=15	2	2x5=10	3	1	3	2x5=10	2	1	2	1	1	2x5=100	2	3x5=15	4	1x5=5	2	1	2	2	2	89
2.	Thakurganj	1	2	4x5=20	1	2x5=10	1	2	4	1x5=5	2	1	2	2	1	1x5=5	2	1x5=5	3	1x5=5	1	1	1	2	1	81
3.	Birpur	1	2	4x5=20	2	0x5=0	2	2	4	3x5=15	0	0	2	1	2	1x5=5	2	2x5=10	3	1x5=5	1	1	2	1	1	85
4.	Maharajganj	2	2	4x5=20	2	0x5=0	3	2	0	1x5=5	0	0	3	1	1	1x5=5	2	2x5=10	4	1x5=5	1	1	1	2	1	73
5.	Chakia	2	2	4x5=20	2	2x5=10	2	1	0	1x5=5	2	1	3	1	2	1x5=5	2	2x5=10	3	1x5=5	1	1	2	2	2	86
6.	Jainagar	2	2	3x5=15	1	1x5=5	2	1	3	2x5=10	2	1	3	1	1	2x5=10	2	3x5=15	3	1x5=5	1	2	1	2	1	91
7.	Dalsingsarai	2	2	3x5=15	1	1x5=5	2	2	2	1x5=5	2	2	3	1	1	2x5=10	2	3x5=15	4	1x5=5	1	2	2	2	2	90
8.	Ghoghardiha	1	2	2x5=10	1	2x5=10	1	1	0	2x5=10	2	1	3	1	1	1x5=5	2	2x5=10	3	1x5=5	1	1	1	1	1	74

Source : Data collected From Notified Area Committee Office Personally in The Sample Town During Oct. No.-1996.